Delicious CHICKEN Dishes

KV-493-038

Light, delicious and easy to prepare, chicken, which was once a weekly, monthly or yearly treat, is now an everyday food. Available fresh, frozen, whole or as selected cuts, there is something to suit everyone when it comes to buying chicken. In this book we present you with a variety of recipes to make the most of not only chicken but also turkey, duck, spatchcock (poussin) and quail.

CONTENTS

Soups 2   Starters 6   Main Meals 12

Salads 34   Snacks 40   Quick Meals 46

Leftovers 58   Techniques 62   Ingredients 76

Useful Information 78   Index 79

THE PANTRY SHELF

Unless otherwise stated, the following ingredients used in this book are:

Cream   Double, suitable for whipping

Flour   White flour, plain or standard

Sugar   White sugar

WHAT'S IN A TABLESPOON?

NEW ZEALAND
1 tablespoon =
15 mL OR 3 teaspoons

UNITED KINGDOM
1 tablespoon =
15 mL OR 3 teaspoons

AUSTRALIA
1 tablespoon =
20 mL OR 4 teaspoons

The recipes in this book were tested in Australia where a 20 mL tablespoon is standard. All measures are level.

The tablespoon in the New Zealand and United Kingdom sets of measuring spoons is 15 mL. In many recipes this difference will not matter. For recipes using baking powder, gelatine, bicarbonate of soda, small quantities of flour and cornflour, simply add another teaspoon for each tablespoon specified.

SOUPS

Whether it's a clear consommé or a hearty chicken and vegetable, nothing beats homemade chicken soup. This selection of recipes shows you just how versatile chicken soup can be – there's something to suit all tastes.

Curried Chicken Soup

Creamy Chicken Soup

Chicken Noodle Soup

Chicken and
Avocado Soup

Curried Chicken Soup

CURRIED CHICKEN SOUP

60 g/2 oz butter
2 onions, chopped
2 cloves garlic, crushed
2 large parsnips, chopped
2 stalks celery, chopped
3 tablespoons flour
1 tablespoon curry powder
6 cups/1.5 litres/2½ pt chicken stock
185 g/6 oz fresh or frozen green peas
500 g/1 lb cooked chicken, chopped
250 g/8 oz sour cream
3 tablespoons finely chopped parsley
2 tablespoons chopped fresh dill

1 Melt butter in a large saucepan and cook onions, garlic, parsnips and celery over a low heat for 5-6 minutes or until vegetables are just tender. Stir in flour and curry powder and cook for 1 minute longer.

2 Remove pan from heat and gradually blend in stock. Cook, stirring constantly, over a medium heat for 8-10 minutes or until soup boils and thickens. Reduce heat, stir in peas and chicken and cook for 10 minutes longer.

3 Remove pan from heat, whisk in sour cream, then stir in parsley and dill. Cook, stirring frequently, over a low heat for 3-4 minutes or until soup is heated. Serve immediately.

Serves 6

A hearty soup that only requires crusty bread to make it a complete meal.

CREAMY CHICKEN SOUP

15 g/½ oz butter
1 clove garlic, finely chopped
8 cups/2 litres/3½ pt chicken stock
1 kg/2 lb cooked chicken, finely chopped
2 teaspoons Worcestershire sauce
2 cups/500 mL/16 fl oz cream (double)
freshly ground black pepper
4 tablespoons chopped fresh parsley
4 tablespoons snipped fresh chives

1 Melt butter in a large saucepan and cook garlic over a low heat for 2-3 minutes. Add stock, bring to the boil, then reduce heat to simmering, stir in chicken and Worcestershire sauce, and cook for 2-3 minutes.

2 Stir in cream and season to taste with black pepper. Add parsley and chives and cook over a medium heat for 4-5 minutes or until soup is hot.

Serves 8

Cooked chicken is a quick and easy way to make chicken soup. But remember, do not cook the chicken for too long after adding to the soup or it will end up as unpalatable strings.

CHICKEN NOODLE SOUP

A homemade, well-seasoned, clear chicken broth filled with chicken, vegetables and noodles is a far cry from most of the packet soups you buy in food shops.

4 cups/1 litre/1^3/$_4$ pt chicken stock
1 carrot, cut into matchsticks
1 leek, thinly sliced
125 g/4 oz cooked chicken, chopped
90 g/3 oz round egg noodles, broken into pieces
freshly ground black pepper
4 sprigs fresh coriander

1 Place stock in a large saucepan and bring to the boil. Add carrot and leek, cover, bring to simmering and simmer for 5 minutes or until carrot is tender.

2 Stir in chicken and noodles and cook for 5-10 minutes or until noodles are tender. Season to taste with black pepper. Serve garnished with coriander sprigs.

Serves 4

Chicken Noodle Soup

Chicken and Avocado Soup

CHICKEN AND AVOCADO SOUP

15 g/^{1}/$_2$ oz butter
1 onion, finely chopped
1 large potato, diced
3 cups/750 mL/1^1/$_4$ pt chicken stock
310 g/10 oz canned sweet
corn kernels, drained
375 g/12 oz cooked chicken, chopped
freshly ground black pepper
3 tablespoons cream or
evaporated skim milk
1 avocado, peeled, stoned and diced

1 Melt butter in a large saucepan and cook onion for 2-3 minutes or until soft. Stir in potato and stock, cover, bring to simmering and simmer for 10-15 minutes or until potato is tender.

2 Add corn, chicken and black pepper to taste and cook for 5-6 minutes or until soup is hot. Spoon soup into individual serving bowls. Swirl in cream or milk and top with avocado. Serve immediately.

Serves 4

Chicken and avocados seem to go together like bread and butter, and no more so than in this substantial soup. For a wonderful luncheon, serve the soup with crusty bread and follow with a mixed green salad.

STARTERS

*Chicken is especially popular for pre-dinner and cocktail nibbles.
The recipes in this section lend themselves to being served as
small portions for the first course of a formal dinner party or as
finger food for a more informal occasion.*

Mango Chicken Bites

Oriental Chicken Rolls

Duck with Cherry
Sauce

Chilli Chicken with
Curry Sauce

Bacon and Mushroom
Rolls

Satay Chicken

Spicy Indian Chicken

Mango Chicken Bites

Mango Chicken Bites

1 teaspoon ground cardamom
2 teaspoons ground cumin
$^1/_2$ teaspoon chilli powder
1 teaspoon ground ginger
5 boneless chicken breast fillets,
cut into 2.5 cm/1 in pieces
2 tablespoons oil

MANGO SAUCE
1 cup/315 g/10 oz mango chutney
$^1/_4$ cup/60 mL/2 fl oz cream (double)
1 tablespoon curry powder

Serves 20 as an hors d'oeuvre

1   Place cardamom, cumin, chilli powder and ginger in a bowl and mix to combine. Add chicken and toss to coat with spice mixture. Cover and set aside to marinate at room temperature for 1 hour.

2   Heat oil in a frying pan and cook chicken, stirring, over a medium heat for 5 minutes or until cooked. Remove from pan and drain on absorbent kitchen paper.

3   To make sauce, place chutney, cream and curry powder in a food processor or blender and process to combine. Serve as a dipping sauce with chicken.

As a starter for a formal meal you might like to arrange the chicken pieces on a bed of mixed lettuce leaves with slices of fresh or canned mango. The Mango Sauce could be served in individual pots on the side of each plate.

Oriental Chicken Rolls

15g/$^1/_2$ oz Chinese dried mushrooms
boiling water
4 spring onions, chopped
60 g/2 oz fresh or frozen peas
freshly ground black pepper
2 boneless chicken breast fillets, cut into
12 strips lengthwise
12 sheets rice paper, cut in half
oil for deep frying

PLUM SAUCE
$^1/_2$ cup/125 mL/4 fl oz plum sauce
2 tablespoons water
2 tablespoons finely chopped cucumber

Makes 24 rolls

1   Place mushrooms in a bowl and cover with boiling water. Set aside to soak for 20 minutes or until mushrooms are tender. Drain, remove stalks and chop mushrooms.

2   Place mushrooms, spring onions and peas in a bowl and mix to combine. Season to taste with black pepper.

3   Place a chicken strip and 2 teaspoons mushroom mixture on a corner of each sheet of rice paper, tuck in edges and roll up. Seal, using a little water. Heat oil in a large saucepan and cook 3-4 rolls at a time for 2-3 minutes or until cooked – the rolls will not brown. Remove rolls from oil and drain on absorbent kitchen paper.

4   To make sauce, place plum sauce, water and cucumber in a bowl and mix to combine. Serve with hot rolls.

Chinese dried mushrooms are available from oriental food shops. They are quite expensive, but keep indefinitely. As their flavour is very strong, only small quantities are used.

DUCK WITH CHERRY SAUCE

2 tablespoons seasoned flour
1 teaspoon five spice powder
750 g/1¹/₂ lb boneless duck breast fillets,
cut into 2.5 cm/1 in pieces
oil for deep frying

CHERRY SAUCE
1 tablespoon sugar
375 g/12 oz canned black cherries,
drained
¹/₃ cup/90 mL/3 fl oz red wine
¹/₄ teaspoon mixed spice

Bite-sized pieces of spicy crisp duck are even more delicious when dipped in Cherry Sauce.

Serves 10 as an hors d'oeuvre

1   Place flour and five spice powder in a plastic food bag and shake to combine. Add duck and shake to coat all pieces.

2   Heat oil in a large saucepan and cook duck in batches for 3-4 minutes or until cooked and golden. Drain on absorbent kitchen paper.

3   To make sauce, place sugar, cherries, red wine and mixed spice in a saucepan. Bring to simmering and simmer, uncovered, for 15 minutes. Press cherry mixture through a sieve, return sieved sauce to a clean saucepan and heat gently for 3-4 minutes or until warm. Serve warm as a dipping sauce with hot duck.

CHILLI CHICKEN WITH CURRY SAUCE

6 boneless chicken breast fillets, cut into
2.5 cm/1 in pieces
¹/₃ cup/90 mL/3 fl oz vegetable oil
2 teaspoons paprika
¹/₂ teaspoon chilli powder
oil for deep frying

CURRY SAUCE
1 tablespoon oil
1 onion, finely chopped
2 teaspoons mild curry powder
1 tablespoon flour
1¹/₄ cups/315 mL/10 fl oz milk
2 tablespoons mango chutney
freshly ground black pepper

Chilli-coated chicken pieces are delicious served with drinks or as a snack.

Serves 10 as an hors d'oeuvre

1   Place chicken, vegetable oil, paprika and chilli powder in a bowl and mix to combine. Cover and set aside to marinate for 1 hour.

2   Heat oil in a large saucepan and cook chicken in batches for 3-4 minutes or until golden and cooked. Drain on absorbent kitchen paper.

3   To make sauce, heat oil in a saucepan and cook onion for 4-5 minutes or until soft. Stir in curry powder and cook for 2 minutes. Add flour and cook, stirring, for 1 minute longer. Gradually stir in milk and bring to the boil, stirring constantly, over a medium heat. Cook for 3-4 minutes or until sauce thickens, then reduce heat and simmer for 5 minutes longer. Stir in chutney and season to taste with black pepper. Serve warm as a dipping sauce with hot chicken.

BACON AND MUSHROOM ROLLS

60 g/2 oz butter
1 onion, finely chopped
185 g/6 oz bacon, chopped
500 g/1 lb chicken livers, trimmed
and chopped
250 g/8 oz mushrooms, chopped
$^{1}/_{2}$ cup/125 mL/4 fl oz chicken stock
2 egg yolks, lightly beaten
$^{1}/_{2}$ teaspoon mixed dried herbs
freshly ground black pepper
4 sheets filo pastry
1 egg white
oil for deep frying

1   Melt butter in a large frying pan and cook onion for 2-3 minutes or until soft. Add bacon and cook for 3-4 minutes longer. Stir in chicken livers and cook, stirring, for 3 minutes or until livers change colour. Add mushrooms and cook for 3 minutes longer.

2   Stir in stock, bring to simmering and simmer for 5 minutes or until almost all stock has evaporated. Remove pan from heat and set aside to cool for 10 minutes.

3   Mix egg yolks, mixed herbs and black pepper to taste into chicken liver mixture. Place chicken liver mixture in a food processor and process to roughly chop. Take care not to make a purée.

4   Cut pastry into twenty-four 15 cm/6 in squares. Place 2 teaspoons of chicken liver mixture on each pastry square, fold in two edges and roll up like a spring roll. Seal edges with a little egg white.

5   Heat oil in a large saucepan and cook 3-4 rolls at a time for 2-3 minutes or until golden. Remove rolls from oil and drain on absorbent kitchen paper.

Makes 24 rolls

Duck with Cherry Sauce,
Bacon and Mushroom Rolls,
Chilli Chicken with Curry Sauce

These crispy rolls filled with chicken livers and mushrooms can be prepared in advance, leaving only the final cooking until just prior to serving. Serve with chilli sauce and soy sauce as dipping condiments.

SATAY CHICKEN

4 boneless chicken breast fillets, cut
into 2 cm/³/4 in cubes

SATAY MARINADE
¹/2 cup/125 mL/4 fl oz water
2 tablespoons peanut butter
1 tablespoon honey
1 tablespoon soy sauce
2 tablespoons lemon juice
1 teaspoon chilli paste (sambal oelek)
1 teaspoon grated fresh ginger
1 onion, finely chopped

One of the most popular of
all Asian dishes, these
chicken satays will disappear
as quickly as you serve them.

Satay Chicken

Makes approximately 20 skewers

1   To make marinade, place water,
peanut butter, honey, soy sauce, lemon
juice, chilli paste (sambal oelek), ginger
and onion in a bowl, and mix to
combine.

2   Add chicken to marinade, toss to
coat, cover and refrigerate for at least 2
hours or overnight. Remove chicken from
marinade and reserve marinade. Thread 2
pieces of chicken onto wooden
toothpicks and cook under a preheated
grill for 5 minutes or until cooked.

3   Place reserved marinade in a saucepan
and bring to the boil. Reduce heat and
simmer for 10 minutes or until marinade
reduces and thickens slightly. Serve hot
as a dipping sauce with chicken.

SPICY INDIAN CHICKEN

**8 boneless chicken breast fillets, cut into
2.5 cm/1 in cubes
1 cup/200 g/6^1/$_2$ oz natural yogurt
1 clove garlic, crushed
1 teaspoon grated fresh ginger
^{1}/$_2$ teaspoon garam masala
^{1}/$_4$ teaspoon turmeric
^{1}/$_4$ teaspoon ground cumin
1 tablespoon chopped fresh coriander
freshly ground black pepper**

CUCUMBER CORIANDER DIP
**^{1}/$_2$ cucumber, grated and drained
1 tablespoon chopped fresh coriander
^{1}/$_2$ cup/100 g/3^1/$_2$ oz natural yogurt
^{1}/$_4$ cup/60 mL/2 fl oz cream (double)
freshly ground black pepper**

1   Place chicken, yogurt, garlic, ginger,
garam masala, turmeric, cumin, coriander
and black pepper to taste in a bowl and
toss to combine. Cover and refrigerate for
at least 4 hours or overnight.

2   Remove chicken from yogurt mixture
and place in a single layer on a lightly
greased baking tray. Cook under a
preheated grill, for 5 minutes or until
cooked. Spear 1 or 2 pieces of chicken
onto wooden toothpicks.

3   To make dip, squeeze excess liquid
from cucumber. Place cucumber,
coriander, yogurt, cream and black pepper
to taste in a bowl and mix to combine.
Serve with chicken for dipping.

Serves 8

Instead of cutting the
chicken fillets into pieces,
marinate them whole, then
grill and serve with rice and
salad for a tasty meal.

11

MAIN MEALS

Feta Drumsticks

Coconut Curry

Rice-filled Chicken

Chicken with Corn

Almond Chicken Rolls

Chicken Bean Bake

Honey-glazed Duck

Spatchcock with Olives

Blueberry Duck

Chicken Marsala

Quail with Olive Rice

Oriental Stir-fry

Herb Chutney Chicken

Pimento Chicken Pie

Chicken Roll Casserole

Honeyed Roast Quail

Chicken Terrine

Avocado Strudel

Chicken Biryani

Chicken Pot Pie

Herbed Spatchcock

Redcurrant Duck

Chickpea Ragout

Grilled, casseroled, fried, baked or roasted, chicken is a family favourite. Cooks love it because it is quick and easy to prepare, can be unadorned or dressed up and combines with many different flavours. These recipes for all kinds of birds are sure to give you many new ideas.

Feta Drumsticks

30 g/1 oz butter
1 clove garlic, crushed
1 bunch English spinach, finely shredded
2 slices ham, finely chopped
125 g/4 oz feta cheese, broken into small pieces
1 teaspoon ground coriander
3 teaspoons ground nutmeg
freshly ground black pepper
12 chicken drumsticks
2 tablespoons olive oil

1 Melt butter in a frying pan and cook garlic over a medium heat for 1 minute. Stir in half the spinach and cook for 3-4 minutes or until spinach is wilted. Remove cooked spinach from pan and set aside. Cook remaining spinach in the same way.

2 Place spinach, ham, feta cheese, coriander, 1 teaspoon nutmeg and black pepper to taste in a bowl and mix to combine. Ease skin carefully away from a drumstick to form a pocket. Place a spoonful of spinach mixture in pocket and pull skin over. Repeat with remaining spinach mixture and drumsticks. Brush drumsticks with oil, sprinkle with remaining nutmeg and place in a baking dish. Bake for 30 minutes or until drumsticks are cooked through.

Serves 6

Oven temperature
180°C, 350°F, Gas 4

These drumsticks are just as good cold or hot. Any leftovers are sure to be popular in packed lunches. If cooked the day before, they are perfect picnic fare.

Coconut Curry

1 tablespoon oil
4 boneless chicken breast fillets, skin removed and halved
2 onions, cut into eighths
2 cloves garlic, chopped
2 tablespoons curry paste
1$\frac{1}{2}$ cups/375 mL/12 fl oz water
3 potatoes, cut into cubes
3 carrots, sliced
2 stalks fresh lemon grass, bruised, or
1 teaspoon finely grated lemon rind
1 tablespoon cornflour
$\frac{1}{2}$ cup/125 mL/4 fl oz coconut milk

1 Heat oil in a large saucepan and cook chicken for 3-4 minutes or until brown on both sides. Remove chicken from pan and set aside. Add onions and garlic to pan and cook over a medium heat for 4-5 minutes or until onions are soft. Stir in curry paste and cook for 1 minute longer.

2 Return chicken to pan and stir in water, potatoes, carrots and lemon grass or lemon rind. Bring to the boil, then reduce heat, cover and simmer for 30 minutes or until chicken and vegetables are tender.

3 Whisk cornflour into coconut milk. Stir coconut milk mixture into chicken and cook, stirring, over a medium heat for 4-5 minutes or until curry boils and thickens. Cook for 3 minutes longer. Just prior to serving, remove lemon grass.

If commercially made coconut milk is unavailable, you can make it using desiccated coconut and water. To make coconut milk, place 500 g/1 lb desiccated coconut in a bowl and pour over 3 cups/ 750 mL/1$\frac{1}{4}$ pt of boiling water. Leave to stand for 30 minutes, then strain, squeezing the coconut to extract as much liquid as possible. This will make a thick coconut milk. The coconut can be used again to make a weaker coconut milk.

Feta Drumsticks

Serves 4

RICE-FILLED CHICKEN

Oven temperature
180°C, 350°F, Gas 4

1 x 1.5 kg/3 lb chicken, cleaned
4 rashers bacon, chopped
4 spring onions, chopped
2 teaspoons curry powder
$^3/4$ cup/170 g/$5^1/2$ oz long-grain
rice, cooked
1 cup/60 g/2 oz bread crumbs,
made from stale bread
1 tablespoon olive oil

MUSHROOM SAUCE
30 g/1 oz butter
1 onion, chopped
1 green pepper, chopped
125 g/4 oz mushrooms, sliced
440 g/14 oz canned tomatoes,
undrained and mashed
2 tablespoons tomato paste (purée)
3 tablespoons red wine
1 tablespoon sugar
$^1/2$ cup/125 mL/4 fl oz water
freshly ground black pepper

1   Using absorbent kitchen paper, pat chicken dry inside and out. Cook bacon, spring onions and curry powder in a frying pan over a medium heat for 4-5 minutes or until bacon is crisp. Remove pan from heat and stir in rice and bread crumbs.

2   Fill cavity of chicken with rice mixture and secure opening with metal or bamboo skewers. Tuck wings under body of chicken and tie legs together. Place bird breast side up in a baking dish. Brush with oil and bake, basting frequently with pan juices, for $1^1/2$ hours or until bird is cooked.

3   To make sauce, melt butter in a saucepan and cook onion, green pepper and mushrooms for 2-3 minutes. Stir in tomatoes, tomato paste (purée), wine, sugar, water and black pepper to taste. Cook, stirring constantly, over a medium heat for 10-15 minutes or until sauce is reduced by a quarter. Serve sauce with chicken.

Serves 4

To test when a bird is cooked, place a skewer into the thickest part of the thigh and when the skewer is removed the juices should run clear. If the juices are tinged pink, return bird to the oven and cook for 15 minutes longer, then test again. On completion of cooking, allow whole birds to stand in a warm place for 10-20 minutes before carving. This tenderises the meat by allowing the juices to settle into the flesh.

CHICKEN WITH CORN

Oven temperature
180°C, 350°F, Gas 4

1 tablespoon olive oil
2 onions, chopped
2 teaspoons ground cumin
4 chicken thighs
4 chicken drumsticks
1 cup/250 mL/8 fl oz dry white wine
1 cup/250 mL/8 fl oz chicken stock
1 cup/250 mL/8 fl oz cream (double)
315 g/10 oz canned sweet corn
kernels, drained

1   Heat oil in a large frying pan and cook onions and cumin over a medium heat for 4-5 minutes or until onions are soft. Add chicken and cook for 8-10 minutes longer or until brown on all sides. Transfer onions and chicken to a casserole dish.

2   Drain fat from pan and stir in wine. Bring to the boil, stirring and scraping bits from base of pan. Boil for 4-5 minutes or until reduced by half.

3   Stir stock, cream and corn into wine and cook for 5 minutes longer. Pour wine mixture over chicken, cover and bake for 45-60 minutes or until chicken is cooked.

Serves 4

Serve this rich cumin-flavoured chicken and corn on a bed of boiled rice and accompany with a green vegetable such as beans, asparagus or spinach.

14

Rice-filled Chicken

ALMOND CHICKEN ROLLS

4 boneless chicken breast fillets,
skin removed
vegetable oil for deep frying

BREAD CRUMB COATING
2 eggs
^{1}/$_3$ cup/90 mL/3 fl oz milk
^{1}/$_2$ cup/60 g/2 oz seasoned flour
2 cups/125 g/4 oz bread crumbs,
made from stale bread

HERB BUTTER
185 g/6 oz butter, softened
60 g/2 oz almonds, chopped
2 teaspoons French mustard
1 tablespoon chopped fresh parsley
1 tablespoon snipped fresh chives
freshly ground black pepper

Do not allow the oil to become too hot when cooking these rolls or the coating will brown before the chicken is cooked.

1   To make Herb Butter, place butter, almonds, mustard, parsley, chives and black pepper to taste in a bowl and mix to combine. Divide butter into four portions and shape into rolls 10 cm/4 in long. Wrap rolls in plastic food wrap and refrigerate until firm.

2   Place fillets between two sheets of plastic food wrap and pound, using a rolling pin, to flatten. Take care not to make holes in the fillets or the butter will run out during cooking.

3   Place a butter roll in the centre of each chicken fillet. Fold the shorter ends of the fillets into the centre, then roll up to fully encase the butter. Secure fillets with toothpicks.

4   To coat, place eggs and milk in a small bowl and beat to combine. Transfer to a shallow dish. Place flour and bread crumbs on separate plates. Coat chicken rolls with flour, then dip in egg mixture and roll in bread crumbs. Repeat egg and bread crumb steps. Place rolls on a plate, cover with plastic food wrap and refrigerate for 1 hour.

5   Heat oil in a large saucepan and cook chicken rolls for 5-8 minutes or until golden and cooked through.

Serves 4

Almond Chicken Rolls

CHICKEN BEAN BAKE

1 rasher bacon, chopped
1.5 kg/3 lb chicken pieces, skin removed
2 onions, chopped
1 clove garlic, crushed
$^1/_2$ cup/125 mL/4 fl oz chicken stock
$^1/_3$ cup/90 mL/3 fl oz white wine
1 teaspoon dried mixed herbs
1 teaspoon sugar
440 g/14 oz canned tomatoes, undrained and mashed
315 g/10 oz canned lima or butter beans, drained

1   Cook bacon in a frying pan, over a medium heat for 2-3 minutes or until crisp. Remove bacon from pan and drain on absorbent kitchen paper.

2   Cook chicken in frying pan for 5-8 minutes or until brown on all sides. Remove chicken from pan and place in a casserole.

3   Add onions and garlic to pan and cook for 2-3 minutes or until onion is soft. Scatter onion mixture and bacon over chicken pieces.

4   Stir stock, wine, herbs, sugar and tomatoes into pan and bring to the boil over a medium heat. Cook, stirring occasionally, until mixture reduces and thickens. Stir in beans and pour over chicken. Cover and bake for 45-60 minutes or until chicken is cooked.

Oven temperature
200°C, 400°F, Gas 6

When cooking poultry pieces, remember that the breast – the white meat – cooks more quickly than the legs and thighs – the dark meat. Cooking the leg and thigh portions for 10 minutes before adding the breast portions will give you evenly cooked poultry pieces.

Chicken Bean Bake   ***Serves 6***

HONEY-GLAZED DUCK

Oven temperature
180°C, 350°F, Gas 4

As a general rule, a 2.5 kg/ 5 lb duck will serve 4 people. Pierce the skin of the duck before cooking and place on a rack set in a baking dish, so that the fat from the duck drains off during cooking.

1 x 2.5 kg/5 lb duck, cleaned
2 onions, halved
5 sprigs fresh parsley

HONEY GLAZE
3 tablespoons honey
1 tablespoon mild mustard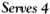
$^1/_4$ cup/60 mL/2 fl oz dry sherry

1   To make glaze, place honey and mustard in a small saucepan and cook, stirring, over a medium heat until honey melts. Stir in sherry and bring to the boil, reduce heat and simmer for 2 minutes. Remove pan from heat and set aside.

2   Place onions and parsley in cavity of duck and secure opening with metal or bamboo skewers. Tuck wings under body of duck and tie legs together. Place bird breast side up on a wire rack, set in a baking dish. Brush duck with glaze and bake, turning several times, for 1 hour or until duck is cooked.

Honey-glazed Duck

Serves 4

Spatchcock with Olives

SPATCHCOCK WITH OLIVES

2 x 500 g/1 lb spatchcocks (poussins)
2 tablespoons olive oil
1 teaspoon cracked black pepper
2 teaspoons dried mixed herbs

BLACK OLIVE STUFFING
60 g/2 oz butter
4 spring onions, finely chopped
6 rashers bacon, finely chopped
90 g/3 oz olives, pitted and chopped
1 cup/60 g/2 oz bread crumbs,
made from stale bread
1 tablespoon chopped fresh thyme or
1 teaspoon dried thyme

1   To make stuffing, melt butter in a frying pan and cook spring onions and bacon over a medium heat for 2 minutes. Remove pan from heat, add olives, bread crumbs and thyme and mix to combine.

2   Fill cavity of each spatchcock (poussin) with stuffing and secure opening with metal or bamboo skewers. Tuck wings under body of bird, tie legs together and place in a baking dish.

3   Brush birds with oil, sprinkle with black pepper and herbs and bake for 45-60 minutes or until birds are cooked.

Serves 2

Oven temperature
180°C, 350°F, Gas 4

A spatchcock, or poussin, is a young chicken weighing 500-900 g/1-2 lb. It has a delicate flesh and is delicious roasted, grilled, pan-cooked or barbecued. Usually one bird is allowed per serving.

19

BLUEBERRY DUCK

Blueberries are used in this recipe, but any other berry fruit can be used instead.

2 tablespoons vegetable oil
4 duck breasts, with skin
3 tablespoons balsamic or
red wine vinegar
¹/₄ teaspoon ground cinnamon
4 tablespoons fresh blueberries
freshly ground black pepper
ZUCCHINI (COURGETTE)
FLOWERS
³/₄ cup/90 g/3 oz flour
1 cup/250 mL/8 fl oz water
vegetable oil for deep frying
12 zucchini (courgette) flowers

1 Heat oil in a large frying pan and cook duck, skin side down, over a low heat for 4-5 minutes or until skin is golden. Turn and cook other side for 3-4 minutes.

2 Add vinegar, cinnamon, blueberries and black pepper to taste. Cover and cook over a low heat for 15 minutes or until duck is tender.

3 To prepare flowers, gradually sift flour into water and mix with a fork until batter is smooth. If necessary, add more water. Pour 2.5 cm/1 in oil into a frying pan and heat until very hot. Dip flowers into batter and cook a few at a time in oil until golden.

4 To serve, arrange duck and flowers on a serving plate and spoon blueberry sauce over duck.

Serves 4

In Italy, zucchini (courgette) flowers are used in many ways. They can be dipped in batter and fried, or stuffed and then fried or used in risotto. If zucchini (courgette) flowers are unavailable, do not be put off making this dish – the duck is just as good served with a green vegetable such as asparagus, beans or zucchini (courgettes).

CHICKEN MARSALA

4 boneless chicken breast fillets,
pounded
3 tablespoons seasoned flour
30 g/1 oz butter
2 tablespoons olive oil
³/₄ cup/185 mL/6 fl oz dry Marsala
or sherry
¹/₃ cup/90 mL/3 fl oz chicken stock
30 g/1 oz butter, softened
freshly ground black pepper

1 Coat chicken in flour and shake off excess. Heat butter and oil in a large frying pan, until butter is foaming. Add chicken and cook for 3 minutes each side.

2 Stir in Marsala or sherry, bring to the boil, reduce heat and simmer for 15 minutes or until chicken is cooked. Remove chicken and set aside to keep warm. Add stock, bring to the boil and boil for 2 minutes. Whisk in softened butter and season to taste with black pepper. To serve, spoon sauce over chicken.

Serves 4

To pound chicken breast fillets, place fillets between two sheets of plastic food wrap and pound, using a rolling pin, to flatten. Take care not to make holes in the fillets. This method of pounding also prevents the fillets from sticking to the pounding utensil.

Quail with Olive Rice, Blueberry Duck,
Chicken Marsala

QUAIL WITH OLIVE RICE

1 tablespoon olive oil
30 g/1 oz butter
2 onions, chopped
2 cloves garlic, crushed
8 quails
5 fresh sage leaves
3 teaspoons chopped fresh rosemary or
1 teaspoon dried rosemary
freshly ground black pepper
1¼ cups/315 mL/10 fl oz dry sherry
OLIVE RICE
375 g/12 oz rice, cooked
60 g/2 oz butter, chopped
6 slices mortadella, chopped
90 g/3 oz pitted black olives, chopped
3 tablespoons grated fresh
Parmesan cheese
3 tablespoons chopped fresh basil

1   Heat oil and butter in a frying pan and cook onions and garlic over a low heat for 3 minutes or until onions are soft.

2   Add quails to pan and cook over a high heat until brown on all sides. Add sage, rosemary and black pepper to taste.

3   Stir in sherry, bring to the boil, then reduce heat and simmer for 20 minutes or until quails are cooked.

4   To prepare rice, place rice, butter, mortadella and olives in a saucepan and cook, stirring, over a low heat for 4-5 minutes until butter is melted and mixture is hot. Mix in Parmesan cheese and basil. To serve, divide rice between four serving plates, top with quails and spoon a little of the pan juices over.

Serves 4

How do you eat quail? In your fingers.
Just as eating asparagus in your fingers is considered permissible, the same goes for quail. In fact, eating quail any other way is very difficult and you leave behind much of the delicious meat.

ORIENTAL STIR-FRY

2 tablespoons vegetable oil
2 onions, cut into eighths
1 clove garlic, crushed
1 teaspoon grated fresh ginger
8 boneless chicken breast fillets,
cut into strips
¼ teaspoon ground cumin
¼ teaspoon ground coriander
3 tablespoons oyster sauce
1 teaspoon sesame oil
125 g/4 oz broccoli, cut into florets
125 g/4 oz snow peas (mangetout),
trimmed
1 tablespoon sesame seeds

1   Heat oil in a frying pan or wok and stir-fry onions, garlic and ginger for 2-3 minutes or until onion is soft. Remove from pan and set aside.

2   Add chicken to pan and stir-fry for 3-4 minutes or until chicken changes colour. Place cumin, coriander, oyster sauce and sesame oil in a small bowl, mix to combine, then stir into pan. Return onion mixture to pan, add broccoli and snow peas (mangetout) and stir-fry for 3-4 minutes or until broccoli and snow peas (mangetout) are tender. Sprinkle with sesame seeds and serve immediately.

Serves 4

A quick and easy Asian-style dish with a medley of flavours that is sure to be popular. Serve with boiled rice or noodles for a complete meal.

HERB CHUTNEY CHICKEN

1 x 1.5 kg/3 lb chicken
60 g/2 oz butter, melted
2 cloves garlic, crushed

CHUTNEY STUFFING
2 tablespoons chopped fresh mixed
herbs such as parsley, chives, rosemary,
thyme and oregano
125 g/4 oz grated fresh Parmesan cheese
2 tablespoons fruit chutney
1 egg, lightly beaten
1 cup/60 g/2 oz dried bread crumbs
90 g/3 oz butter, melted

Herb Chutney Chicken

1   To make stuffing, place herbs, Parmesan cheese, chutney, egg, bread crumbs and butter in a bowl and mix to combine. Fill cavity of chicken with stuffing and secure opening with metal or bamboo skewers.

2   Tuck wings under body of chicken and tie legs together. Place bird breast side up in a baking dish. Combine butter and garlic, brush over chicken and bake, turning several times, for 1-1^1/$_2$ hours or until bird is cooked.

Serves 4

Oven temperature
180°C, 350°F, Gas 4

When making stuffing, try doubling the quantity and cooking the remainder in a dish to serve as extra stuffing with the bird. Or use to fill vegetables such as tomatoes and red and green peppers. These vegetables will take 20-30 minutes to cook and can be baked with the chicken.

23

Pimento Chicken Pie

Oven temperature
180°C, 350°F, Gas 4

A chicken pie with a difference. The polenta pastry has a deliciously different texture and the filling is like no other you have tasted. For a complete meal, serve with a salad of mixed lettuces, tomatoes and olives tossed in a light vinaigrette dressing.

POLENTA PASTRY
1$^{1}/_{2}$ cups/375 g/12 oz flour
$^{1}/_{3}$ cup/60 g/2 oz polenta (corn meal)
155 g/5 oz butter, cut into pieces
1 egg, lightly beaten
$^{1}/_{2}$ cup/125 mL/4 fl oz water

CHICKEN PIMENTO FILLING
1 tablespoon olive oil
500 g/1 lb frozen spinach, thawed
2 cloves garlic, crushed
30 g/1 oz pine nuts
5 slices prosciutto or ham, chopped
3 chicken breast fillets, poached and chopped
2 pieces canned pimento or $^{1}/_{2}$ red pepper, cut into strips
3 eggs, lightly beaten
1 cup/250 mL/8 fl oz cream (double)
freshly ground black pepper

1 To make pastry, place flour, polenta and butter in a food processor and process until mixture resembles fine bread crumbs. With machine running, add egg, then water a tablespoon at a time until mixture forms a ball. Turn dough onto a lightly floured surface and knead lightly. Wrap in plastic food wrap and refrigerate for 30 minutes.

2 To make filling, heat oil in a large frying pan and cook spinach, garlic, pine nuts and prosciutto or ham over a medium heat for 4-5 minutes or until pine nuts are golden. Transfer spinach mixture to a bowl and set aside to cool completely. Add chicken, pimento or red pepper, eggs and cream, and mix to combine.

3 Roll out two-thirds of polenta dough on a lightly floured surface and line the base and sides of a lightly greased, deep 23 cm/9 in pie dish. Trim edges using a sharp knife. Spoon filling into pie dish. On a lightly floured surface, roll out remaining pastry large enough to cover pie. Brush edge of pastry with water and cover with pastry top. Press edges together to seal, then trim and make a decorative edge using fingertips. Make two slits in top of pie to allow steam to escape. Bake for 45 minutes or until pastry is golden.

Serves 8

Pimento Chicken Pie

CHICKEN ROLL CASSEROLE

6 boneless chicken breast fillets,
skin removed
3 rashers bacon
1 tablespoon chopped fresh parsley
60 g/2 oz butter
2 onions, chopped
2 carrots, grated
8 spinach leaves
freshly ground black pepper
3 potatoes, cooked
$^1/_2$ cup/125 mL/4 fl oz water

1   Place fillets between two sheets of plastic food wrap and pound, using a rolling pin, to flatten. Remove rind from bacon and cut each rasher in half. Place a piece of bacon on each chicken fillet and sprinkle with parsley. Fold the shorter ends of the fillets into the centre, then roll up and secure fillets with toothpicks.

2   Melt half the butter in a large frying pan and cook chicken rolls for 8-10 minutes or until brown on all sides. Remove rolls from pan and set aside.

3   Melt remaining butter in frying pan and cook onions and carrots, stirring, for 5 minutes or until onions are soft. Add spinach and cook, stirring, for 2-3 minutes longer or until spinach is wilted. Season to taste with black pepper.

4   Cut potatoes into thick slices and place in the base of a casserole dish. Top with vegetable mixture, then chicken rolls. Pour water over, cover and bake for 35-40 minutes or until chicken rolls are cooked.

Serves 6

Oven temperature
180°C, 350°F, Gas 4

Chicken rolls filled with bacon and parsley make a complete meal when teamed with vegetables and cooked in a casserole. Serve with crusty bread rolls or garlic bread.

Chicken Roll Casserole

Honeyed Roast Quail

HONEYED ROAST QUAIL

Oven temperature
180°C, 350°F, Gas 4

Native to the Middle East, the quail is the smallest game bird and is related to the pheasant. It is now reared on farms and considered a gourmet item. Due to the small size of the bird, two are usually considered to be a serving.

4 quails

SOY HONEY GLAZE
1 tablespoon sesame oil
$^1/_4$ cup/60 mL/2 fl oz soy sauce
$^1/_4$ cup/90 g/3 oz honey
2 tablespoons lemon juice
1 tablespoon sesame seeds

1   To make glaze, place oil, soy sauce, honey, lemon juice and sesame seeds in a small saucepan and cook, stirring, over a medium heat for 10 minutes.

2   Tuck wings under body of each quail and tie legs together. Place breast side up in a baking dish and brush with glaze. Bake, basting several times, for 25 minutes or until birds are cooked.

Serves 2

CHICKEN TERRINE

1 x 1.5 kg/3 lb chicken
8 cups/2 litres/3^1/$_2$ pt water
2 carrots, chopped
2 onions, quartered
60 g/2 oz chopped fresh parsley
1 tablespoon black peppercorns
4 bay leaves
1 tablespoon gelatine
^{1}/$_4$ cup/60 mL/2 fl oz boiling water
2 stalks celery, finely chopped
2 spring onions, finely chopped
30 g/1 oz basil leaves, chopped
250 g/8 oz ham slices, chopped

1 Place chicken, water, carrots, onions, parsley, peppercorns and bay leaves in a large saucepan and bring to the boil. Reduce heat and simmer for 2 hours.

2 Remove chicken from cooking liquid and set aside to cool completely. Strain stock into a bowl and discard vegetables.

3 Strip flesh from chicken, discarding skin and bones. Place chicken flesh in a food processor and process to roughly chop. Take care not to process to a paste.

4 Place strained stock in a clean saucepan, bring to the boil, then reduce heat and simmer, uncovered, until stock is reduced to 3 cups/750 mL/1^1/$_4$ pt. Dissolve gelatine in boiling water then stir into hot stock. Set aside to cool slightly.

5 Place celery, spring onions and basil in a bowl, and mix to combine. Place ham in the base of a loaf tin lined with plastic food wrap, then top with celery mixture and finally with chicken. Pour over stock mixture and press down to evenly distribute stock and to immerse chicken. Cover and refrigerate until set. To serve, turn terrine onto a plate and slice.

Serves 8

Ideal for a garden party or even to take on a picnic, this terrine takes time to prepare, but the delicious flavour makes it worthwhile. One shortcut would be to use a barbecued chicken and commercial chicken stock.

Chicken Terrine

AVOCADO STRUDEL

Oven temperature
180°C, 350°F, Gas 4

This recipe is also delicious made with tuna or salmon in place of the chicken. For a lower kilojoule (calorie) version, ricotta cheese can be used instead of cream cheese.

Avocado Strudel

10 sheets filo pastry
4 tablespoons vegetable oil
2 tablespoons sesame seeds

CHICKEN AVOCADO FILLING

1 tablespoon oil
1 small onion, chopped
2 teaspoons curry powder
200 g/6$^1/2$ oz cream cheese, softened
2 chicken breast fillets, cooked
and cut into strips
$^1/2$ red pepper, sliced
8 button mushrooms, sliced
1 avocado, stoned, peeled and sliced
freshly ground black pepper

1 To make filling, heat oil in a frying pan and cook onion and curry powder for 4-5 minutes or until onion is soft. Transfer onion mixture to a bowl, add cream cheese, chicken, red pepper, mushrooms, avocado and black pepper to taste. Mix well to combine.

2 Layer filo pastry sheets on top of each other, brushing between layers with oil. Top pastry with chicken mixture and roll up tightly, tucking ends under. Place on a baking tray, brush with oil, sprinkle with sesame seeds and bake for 30 minutes or until golden.

Serves 6

28

CHICKEN BIRYANI

90 g/3 oz ghee or butter
3 onions, sliced
1.5 kg/3 lb chicken pieces
2 teaspoons grated fresh ginger
3 cloves garlic, crushed
$^1/_2$ teaspoon ground cumin
$^1/_2$ teaspoon ground cinnamon
$^1/_4$ teaspoon ground cloves
$^1/_4$ teaspoon ground cardamom
$^1/_4$ teaspoon ground nutmeg
$^1/_2$ teaspoon flour
1 cup/250 mL/8 fl oz chicken stock
$^1/_2$ cup/100 g/3$^1/_2$ oz natural yogurt
$^1/_2$ cup/125 mL/4 fl oz cream (double)
60 g/2 oz roasted cashew nuts, chopped

RICE PILAU
60 g/2 oz ghee
$^1/_2$ teaspoon ground saffron
$^1/_2$ teaspoon ground cardamom
1 teaspoon salt
1 cup/220 g/7 oz basmati rice,
well-washed
4 cups/1 litre/1$^3/_4$ pt chicken stock
2 tablespoons sultanas

1 Heat ghee or butter in a large frying pan and cook onions, stirring, over a medium heat for 5 minutes or until golden. Remove from pan and set aside.

Add chicken to pan and cook for 3-4 minutes each side or until golden. Remove from pan and set aside.

2 Add ginger, garlic, cumin, cinnamon, cloves, cardamom, nutmeg and flour to pan and cook, stirring, for 1-2 minutes. Add stock, yogurt and cream, stirring to lift sediment from base of pan. Return chicken and half the onion mixture to pan, cover and simmer for 15-20 minutes or until chicken is just cooked. Remove pan from heat and stand, covered, for 15 minutes.

3 To make pilau, melt ghee or butter in a large saucepan and cook saffron, cardamom, salt and rice, stirring constantly, for 1-2 minutes. Add stock and bring to the boil. Stir in sultanas, reduce heat and simmer for 10-15 minutes or until most of the stock is absorbed and rice is cooked. Cover and set aside to stand for 10 minutes.

4 Place rice on a large ovenproof serving platter, top with chicken pieces and spoon sauce over. Sprinkle with remaining onions and cashew nuts, cover and bake for 20 minutes.

Serves 4

Oven temperature
180°C, 350°F, Gas 4

The Great Moguls (Muslim emperors of India between 1526 and 1857) served biryani at lavish feasts on plates so large that two people were required to carry them.

Chicken Biryani

CHICKEN POT PIE

Oven temperature
200°C, 400°F, Gas 6

A delicious herb topping is an imaginative alternative to potatoes in this cobbler-style recipe. Serve with a green vegetable, such as beans, spinach or cabbage, for a complete meal.

60 g/2 oz butter
1 large onion, chopped
4 chicken breast fillets,
cut into 2 cm/³/4 in cubes
2 potatoes, cut into 1 cm/¹/2 in cubes
2 large carrots, cut into
1 cm/¹/2 in cubes
¹/4 cup/30 g/1 oz flour
1 cup/250 mL/8 fl oz dry white wine
3 cups/750 mL/1¹/4 pt chicken stock
1 cup/250 mL/8 fl oz cream (double)
2 tablespoons tomato paste (purée)

HERBED SCONE TOPPING
2 cups/250 g/8 oz self-raising
flour, sifted
1 teaspoon dried mixed herbs
30 g/1 oz grated fresh Parmesan cheese
30 g/1 oz butter, chopped
1 cup/250 mL/8 fl oz milk

1   Melt butter in a large frying pan and cook onion, stirring, over a medium heat for 3-4 minutes or until onion is soft. Add chicken and cook, stirring, for 3 minutes longer.

2   Add potatoes and carrots and cook, stirring, for 8-10 minutes. Stir in flour, then wine, stock, cream and tomato paste (purée), and bring to simmering. Simmer for 10 minutes then transfer mixture to a casserole dish.

3   To make topping, place flour, herbs, Parmesan cheese and butter in a food processor and process to combine. With machine running, add milk and process to form a sticky dough. Turn dough onto a lightly floured surface and knead until smooth. Press dough out to 2 cm/³/4 in thick and, using a scone cutter, cut out rounds and place on top of casserole.

4   Bake for 20-25 minutes or until topping is cooked and golden, and casserole is hot.

Serves 4

Chicken Pot Pie

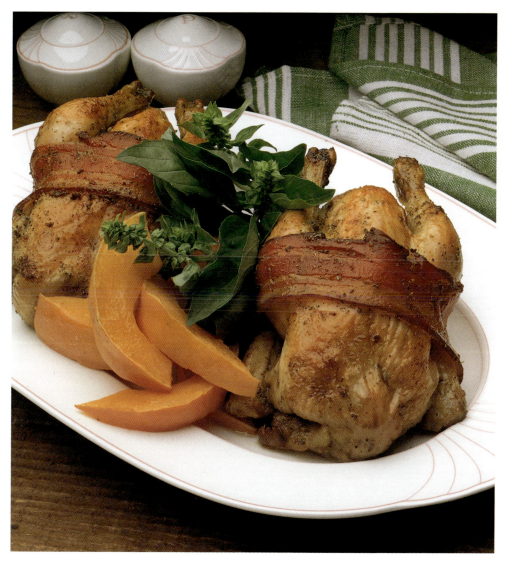

Herbed Spatchcock

HERBED SPATCHCOCK

4 spatchcocks (poussins)
4 sprigs fresh thyme
4 rashers bacon, rind removed

HERB BUTTER MARINADE
1 tablespoon dried mixed herbs
90 g/3 oz butter, melted
3 tablespoons vegetable oil

Serves 4

1   To make marinade, place herbs, butter and oil in a small bowl and mix to combine.

2   Place a sprig of thyme in cavity of each spatchcock. Tuck wings under spatchcocks and tie legs together. Wrap a bacon rasher around each bird and secure with a toothpick. Place birds breast side up in a baking dish, brush with marinade and bake, basting frequently with marinade, for 30-35 minutes or until cooked.

Oven temperature
180°C, 350°F, Gas 4

Delicious served with a tossed salad of mixed lettuce and fresh herbs and crusty wholemeal rolls.

31

REDCURRANT DUCK

2 tablespoons olive oil
8 duck breasts, with skin
^{1}/4 cup/60 mL/2 fl oz fresh lime
or lemon juice
2 tablespoons honey
^{1}/2 cup/170 g/5^1/2 oz redcurrant jelly
125 g/4 oz fresh or frozen redcurrants

Pan-cooked duck breasts
with a redcurrant sauce
make an elegant main
course. Serve with
asparagus, a sauté of leek
strips and new potatoes.

1   Heat oil in a large frying pan and cook
duck breasts for 7-8 minutes each side or
until golden and cooked to your liking.
Remove from pan, set aside and keep
warm.

2   Drain fat from pan and add lime or
lemon juice, honey and redcurrant jelly.
Bring to the boil over a medium heat,
stirring to lift sediment from base of pan.
Reduce heat and simmer for 3-4 minutes
or until mixture reduces and thickens
slightly. Stir in redcurrants and cook,
stirring, for 1 minute longer. Serve sauce

Serves 4   with duck.

CHICKPEA RAGOUT

^{1}/4 cup/60 mL/2 fl oz olive oil
1 onion, chopped
1 teaspoon ground turmeric
1 x 1.5 kg/3 lb chicken, cut
into 6 pieces
220 g/7 oz chickpeas, soaked
overnight, drained
2 cups/500 mL/16 fl oz chicken stock
^{1}/4 cup/60 mL/2 fl oz fresh lemon juice
3 cloves garlic, crushed
30 g/1 oz blanched almonds, toasted
1 tablespoon chopped fresh parsley

Chickpeas take 45-60
minutes to cook. The cooking
time can vary depending on
the quality and age of the
chickpeas and their place of
origin. This recipe could be
made using canned
chickpeas. If using canned
chickpeas, heat oil in a large
frying pan and cook onion,
turmeric, chicken and garlic,
stirring, for 4-5 minutes.
Transfer chicken mixture to a
saucepan and stir in
2 tablespoons lemon juice,
1 cup/250 mL/8 fl oz stock
(the remaining lemon juice
and stock will not be used in
this version of the recipe) and
chickpeas. Bring to
simmering and simmer for
15-20 minutes or until hot. Just
prior to serving, sprinkle with
almonds and parsley.

1   Heat oil in a large frying pan and cook
onion and turmeric, stirring, over a
medium heat for 3 minutes or until onion
is soft. Add chicken pieces and cook for 4
minutes each side or until golden.
Remove chicken pieces from pan and set
aside.

2   Add chickpeas, stock, lemon juice and
garlic to pan, bring to the boil, then
reduce heat and simmer for 40 minutes.
Return chicken to pan and simmer for 20
minutes longer or until chicken and
chickpeas are tender. Just prior to serving,
sprinkle with almonds and parsley.

Serves 4

Redcurrant Duck,
Chickpea Ragout

SALADS

*Served with crusty bread and a salad of mixed
lettuces, chicken salads are the most delicious of summer meals.
In this chapter you will find recipes not only for chicken salads
but also for a marvellous Creamy Roast Duck Salad and an
elegant Spinach and Chicken Liver Salad.*

Fruity Smoked
Chicken Salad

Tomato and
Chicken Salad

Warm Oriental
Chicken Salad

Chicken and
Orange Salad

Spinach and
Chicken Liver Salad

Creamy Roast
Duck Salad

Fruity Smoked Chicken Salad

FRUITY SMOKED CHICKEN SALAD

2 ripe pears, cored and halved vertically
1 x 1.5 kg/3 lb smoked chicken, skin
removed, cut into strips

WATERCRESS DRESSING
30 g/1 oz butter
1 small bunch watercress
4 spring onions, chopped
1 clove garlic, crushed
2 teaspoons tarragon vinegar
1 tablespoon dry white wine
1 cup/250 mL/8 fl oz cream (double)

Serves 4 as a starter or light meal

1   To make dressing, melt butter in a
saucepan, stir in watercress, spring onions,
garlic, vinegar and white wine and bring
to simmering over a medium heat.
Simmer for 5 minutes, then stir in cream
and simmer, uncovered, for 10 minutes
longer or until dressing reduces and
thickens. Remove from heat and set aside
to cool for 10 minutes. Place dressing in a
food processor or blender and process
until smooth. Set aside to cool
completely.

2   Cut each pear half into slices vertically
from the base without cutting through
top. Fan pear and arrange attractively on
plate with chicken. Spoon dressing over
chicken and serve immediately.

Smoked chicken is one of the
more recent food products
and is available from some
supermarkets and
delicatessens. It has been
cured and smoked and has
a pale pink flesh with a
delicate flavour.

TOMATO AND CHICKEN SALAD

1 loaf unsliced wholegrain bread
3 tablespoons olive oil
4 rashers bacon, cut into strips
1 cooked chicken, skin removed and
flesh cut into bite-sized pieces
250 g/8 oz cherry tomatoes,
cut into quarters
2 spring onions, finely chopped
freshly ground black pepper
6 fresh basil sprigs

BASIL MAYONNAISE
1 clove garlic, crushed
60 g/2 oz fresh basil leaves
1 cup/250 g/8 oz mayonnaise

1   Remove crusts from bread and cut
into 2.5 cm/1 in cubes. Place in a bowl
and sprinkle with olive oil. Toss to coat
bread cubes evenly with oil. Arrange
bread cubes in a single layer on a baking
tray and bake for 10-15 minutes or until
golden and toasted. Set aside to cool.

2   Cook bacon in a frying pan for 4-5
minutes or until crisp. Remove bacon
from pan, drain on absorbent kitchen
paper and set aside to cool.

3   To make mayonnaise, place garlic,
basil leaves and 1 tablespoon mayonnaise
in a food processor or blender and process
to purée. Add remaining mayonnaise and
process to combine.

4   Place chicken, tomatoes, spring
onions, black pepper to taste and half the
bacon in a large salad bowl. Top with
mayonnaise and toss to coat all
ingredients. Divide salad between six
plates, place croutons around edge of each
plate, sprinkle with remaining bacon and
garnish with basil sprigs.

Oven temperature
180°C, 350°F, Gas 4

This easy-to-prepare chicken
salad is a main course meal
in itself that needs no other
accompaniment.

Serves 6 as a main meal

WARM ORIENTAL CHICKEN SALAD

220 g/7 oz cellophane or
transparent noodles
boiling water
1 cooked chicken, skin removed
and flesh shredded
1 carrot, grated
3 tablespoons chopped fresh coriander
1 cucumber, chopped
30 g/1 oz peanuts, chopped

PEANUT DRESSING
2 cloves garlic, crushed
$^1/_4$ cup/60 mL/2 fl oz soy sauce
$^1/_4$ cup/60 mL/2 fl oz fresh lemon juice
1 tablespoon peanut butter
$^1/_3$ cup/90 mL/3 fl oz vegetable oil
1 tablespoon brown sugar

The best way to cook a chicken for a chicken salad is to place it breast side down in a saucepan. Pour over enough cold water just to cover the bird. Cut 1 onion into thick slices and add to pan with 4 peppercorns and several sprigs of parsley. Bring to the boil over a medium heat, then reduce heat, cover and simmer for 45 minutes or until chicken is cooked. Transfer chicken and cooking liquid to a large bowl. Ensure that chicken is breast side down in the bowl so that the breast flesh remains moist. Cover and refrigerate until cold.

1 Place noodles in a large heatproof bowl, pour over boiling water to cover and set aside to stand for 10 minutes. Drain.

2 Place chicken, carrot, coriander and cucumber in a bowl and mix to combine.

3 To make dressing, place garlic, soy sauce, lemon juice, peanut butter, oil and sugar in a small saucepan and bring to the boil, stirring, over a medium heat. Cook, stirring, for 3 minutes. Pour dressing over chicken and toss to combine.

4 Divide noodles between four plates, top with chicken mixture and sprinkle with peanuts. Serve immediately.

Serves 4 as a main meal

CHICKEN AND ORANGE SALAD

1 cooked chicken, skin removed and
flesh cut into bite-sized pieces
2 stalks celery, sliced
220 g/7 oz canned water chestnuts,
drained and halved
1 orange, segmented
1 red onion, chopped

TARRAGON DRESSING
1 tablespoon chopped fresh parsley
1/3 cup/90 mL/3 fl oz safflower oil
1 clove garlic, crushed
1/4 cup/60 mL/2 fl oz tarragon vinegar

1   Place chicken, celery, water chestnuts,
orange segments and onion in a salad
bowl. Toss gently to combine.

2   To make dressing, place parsley, oil,
garlic and vinegar in a screwtop jar, and
shake well to combine. Pour over salad
and toss gently.

Serves 4

Chunks of tender chicken,
pieces of crunchy celery and
water chestnuts team with
fresh-tasting orange
segments to make the
perfect summer lunch.

Chicken and Orange Salad

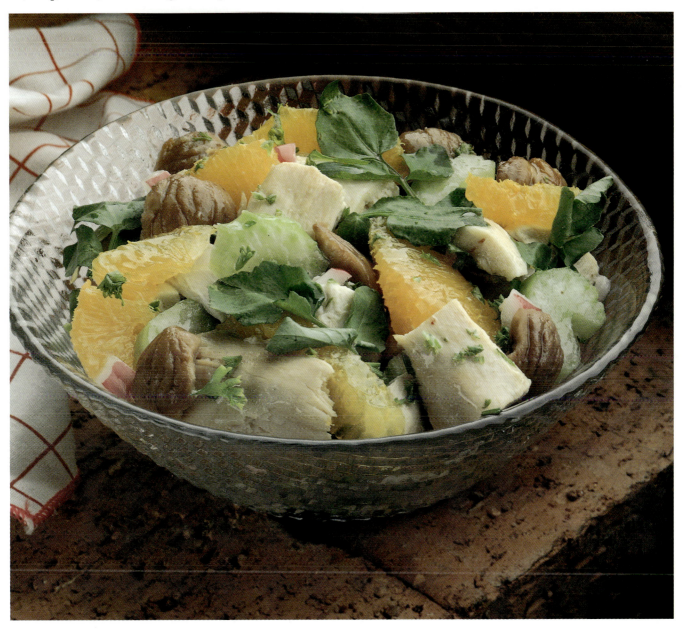

SPINACH AND CHICKEN LIVER SALAD

6 slices white bread, crusts removed
60 g/2 oz butter
250 g/8 oz chicken livers, trimmed
3 tablespoons brandy
1 tablespoon dried mixed herbs
250 g/8 oz spinach, stalks
removed and discarded
$^1/_4$ cup/60 mL/2 fl oz dry white wine
1 tablespoon olive oil
1 red pepper, finely chopped

1   Using biscuit cutters, cut bread into decorative shapes. Melt half the butter in a frying pan over a medium heat until bubbling. Add bread and cook for 1-2 minutes each side or until golden. Remove croutons from pan and drain on absorbent kitchen paper.

2   Melt remaining butter in frying pan and cook chicken livers, stirring constantly, for 2-3 minutes. Add brandy and herbs and cook for 3 minutes longer.

3   Arrange spinach on a large platter or in a salad bowl. Using a slotted spoon remove chicken livers from pan, slice and scatter over spinach. Add wine to pan and cook over a medium heat for 2 minutes, strain mixture into small bowl and discard any sediment. Add oil to strained mixture and mix to combine. Spoon dressing over salad, then top with croutons and red pepper.

Warm chicken livers, pretty-shaped croutons and spinach combine to make an attractive starter.

Spinach and Chicken Liver Salad

Serves 4 as a starter or light meal

CREAMY ROAST DUCK SALAD

1 x 2 kg/4 lb duck
freshly ground black pepper
2 tablespoons chopped fresh parsley

CREAMY ONION DRESSING
2 red onions, cut into wedges
2 tablespoons vegetable oil
³/4 cup/185 mL/6 fl oz chicken stock
¹/2 cup/125 mL/4 fl oz dry white wine
³/4 cup/185 g/6 oz sour cream

1 Season duck with black pepper. Tuck wings under body of duck and tie legs together. Place bird breast side up on a wire rack set in a baking dish and bake for 1 hour or until duck is cooked. Remove from pan and set aside to cool completely.

2 To make dressing, separate onion wedges. Heat oil in a frying pan and cook onions for 5 minutes or until soft. Stir in stock and cook for 8 minutes. Add wine, bring to the boil, then reduce heat and simmer, stirring, to lift sediment from base of pan for 5 minutes. Remove pan from heat, transfer contents to a bowl and set aside to cool to room temperature. Place sour cream in a bowl, add stock mixture and mix well to combine.

3 Remove skin from duck and discard. Strip flesh from duck, cut into bite-sized pieces and place in a bowl. Add dressing and toss to combine. Just prior to serving, sprinkle with parsley. Serve salad at room temperature or chilled.

Serves 4 as a light meal

Oven temperature
180°C, 350°F, Gas 4

Serve this delicious duck salad with boiled new potatoes or a plain rice dish and cold asparagus spears.

Creamy Roast Duck Salad

SNACKS

*Tacos, burgers and open sandwiches are
all wonderful snack foods or light meals. Homemade, using
chicken, they make healthy and nutritious alternatives
to commercial fast foods.*

Chicken Tacos

Bacon and Chicken
Liver Kebabs

Healthy Chicken
Burgers

Chicken and
Pepper Tortillas

Buttermilk Muffins with
Turkey

Grilled Avocado
Sandwiches

Chicken Tacos

CHICKEN TACOS

1 tablespoon vegetable oil
1 large onion, finely chopped
2 cloves garlic, crushed
500 g/1 lb chicken mince
2 tablespoons (30 g/1 oz packet)
taco seasoning mix
$^1/_2$ cup/125 mL/4 fl oz water
3 tablespoons taco sauce
8 taco shells, warmed
60 g/2 oz grated tasty cheese
(mature Cheddar)

1 Heat oil in a large frying pan and cook onion and garlic over a medium heat for 3-4 minutes or until onion is soft. Add chicken and cook, stirring, for 5-6 minutes or until chicken changes colour. Stir in taco seasoning mix, water and taco sauce, bring to simmering and simmer for 4-5 minutes.

2 Divide chicken mixture between taco shells, top with grated cheese and serve with extra taco sauce if desired.

Serves 4

Taco shells are a great store-cupboard item. This recipe could also be made using leftover roast chicken. If using cooked chicken, remove skin, and mince or finely chop chicken. Cook as in recipe but only cook chicken for 2-3 minutes.

BACON AND CHICKEN LIVER KEBABS

500 g/1 lb chicken livers, trimmed
$^3/_4$ cup/185 mL/6 fl oz brandy
2 cloves garlic, crushed
220 g/7 oz bacon, rinds removed

1 Place chicken livers, brandy and garlic in a bowl and toss to combine. Cover and set aside to marinate for 1 hour. Drain chicken livers. Cut bacon rashers in half and wrap around each liver.

2 Thread three bacon-wrapped livers onto lightly oiled bamboo skewers and cook under a preheated grill for 2 minutes each side or until bacon is crisp and livers are cooked.

Serves 4

When cooking chicken livers, take care not to overcook them or they will be dry and tough. Perfectly cooked chicken liver should still be slightly pink inside.

Healthy Chicken Burgers

HEALTHY CHICKEN BURGERS

4 thick slices tomato
4 hamburger buns, split and toasted
8 slices cucumber
4 lettuce leaves
30 g/1 oz alfalfa sprouts

CHICKEN PATTIES
500 g/1 lb chicken mince
1 egg, lightly beaten
$^1/_2$ cup/30 g/1 oz bread crumbs,
made from stale bread
2 teaspoons Worcestershire sauce
30 g/1 oz butter

1   To make patties, place chicken mince, egg, bread crumbs and Worcestershire sauce in a bowl and mix to combine. Shape mixture into eight patties, place on a plate, cover and refrigerate for 20-30 minutes.

2   Melt butter in a large frying pan and cook patties, pressing down with a spatula, for 3-4 minutes each side or until cooked. Remove patties from pan and drain on absorbent kitchen paper.

3   To assemble burgers, place a tomato slice on the bottom half of each bun, top with 2 patties, 2 cucumber slices, a lettuce leaf, a few alfalfa sprouts and top half of bun. Serve immediately.

Serves 4

A burger made with lots of healthy salad ingredients and a patty of lean chicken is just the right snack or light meal for weekend fare.
If you cannot purchase chicken mince, you can make your own using 500 g/ 1 lb boneless chicken breast fillets. Remove skin from fillets before mincing.

CHICKEN AND PEPPER TORTILLAS

3 tablespoons tomato paste (purée)
125 g/4 oz grated tasty cheese
(mature Cheddar)
250 g/8 oz chopped cooked chicken
1/2 green pepper, chopped
1 fresh red chilli, seeds removed
and chopped

TORTILLAS
1^1/2 cups/250 g/8 oz polenta (corn meal)
1^1/2 cups/375 g/12 oz flour
pinch salt
75 g/2^1/2 oz butter, chopped
^{3}/4 cup/185 mL/6 fl oz warm water

1   To make Tortillas, place polenta (corn meal), flour, salt and butter in a food processor and process until mixture resembles fine bread crumbs. With machine running, slowly add water to form a dough. Turn dough onto a lightly floured surface and knead for 2 minutes.

2   Roll out dough and, using a 10 cm/4 in round cutter, cut out eight circles. Place rounds on a lightly greased baking tray and bake for 10 minutes.

3   Spread each tortilla with tomato paste (purée), sprinkle with cheese, chicken, green pepper and chilli and bake for 10 minutes.

Makes 8 tortillas

Oven temperature
180°C, 350°F, Gas 4

In Mexico, thin pancakes made of corn meal are called tortillas, while in Spain a tortilla is a flat omelette.

Chicken and Pepper Tortillas

BUTTERMILK MUFFINS WITH TURKEY

Oven temperature
180°C, 350°F, Gas 4

Buttermilk is a cultured dairy product that has the same food value as skim milk. It is a useful low-fat ingredient that is sometimes used in baked goods.

60 g/2 oz butter
250 g/8 oz sliced smoked turkey
$^1/_2$ cup/155 g/5 oz guava, apple or redcurrant jelly

BUTTERMILK MUFFINS
125 g/4 oz butter
$^1/_2$ cup/100 g/3$^1/_2$ oz caster sugar
2 eggs
60 g/2 oz sultanas, chopped
60 g/2 oz walnuts, chopped
1 teaspoon bicarbonate of soda
1 cup/250 mL/8 fl oz buttermilk or milk
2 cups/250 g/8 oz flour, sifted

1 To make muffins, place butter and sugar in a bowl and beat until creamy. Add eggs, one at a time, beating well after each addition. Stir in sultanas and walnuts. Dissolve bicarbonate of soda in buttermilk or milk. Fold flour and milk mixture, alternately, into creamed mixture.

2 Spoon batter into greased muffin pans and cook for 12 minutes or until golden and cooked when tested with a skewer. Turn on a wire rack to cool.

3 Split muffins, spread lightly with butter. Top bottom half with turkey slices, guava jelly and top of muffin.

Makes 15 muffins

Buttermilk Muffins with Turkey

Grilled Avocado Sandwiches

GRILLED AVOCADO SANDWICHES

4 thick slices brown bread
60 g/2 oz cream cheese, softened
4 tablespoons mayonnaise
250 g/8 oz cooked chicken, sliced
4 slices tasty cheese (mature Cheddar)
1 avocado, stoned, peeled and sliced
1 tablespoon snipped fresh chives

1   Spread each slice of bread with cream cheese, then mayonnaise. Top with chicken and a cheese slice. Cook under a preheated grill for 2-3 minutes or until cheese melts.

2   Top with avocado slices, sprinkle with chives and serve immediately.

Serves 4

QUICK MEALS

Chicken is ideal for those times when a substantial meal is required but time is short. This chapter provides recipes to fit that bill perfectly. It is filled with wonderful ideas for quick family meals and impromptu entertaining.

Chicken Waldorf Loaf

Crusty Parmesan
Drumsticks

Turkey Croquettes

Summer Chicken
Sauté

Chicken with Curry
Sauce

Grilled Honey Chicken

Redcurrant
Spatchcock

Chinese Chicken
Wings

Chicken Stroganoff

Chicken and Pimento
Casserole

Vegetable Pan-fry

Chicken and
Vegetable Pancakes

Chicken Waldorf Loaf

CHICKEN WALDORF LOAF

1 cottage loaf
1 Granny Smith apple, finely chopped
60 g/2 oz walnuts, chopped
3 spring onions, finely chopped
2 tablespoons chopped fresh parsley
1/2 cup/125 g/4 oz mayonnaise
freshly ground black pepper
10 spinach leaves, stalks removed
and discarded
3 boneless chicken breast fillets,
cooked and sliced
4 tomatoes, sliced

1   Cut top off the loaf and scoop out middle, so that only the crust remains as a large bread case. Reserve top of loaf. The crumbs from the centre will not be used in this recipe, but can be made into bread crumbs.

2   Place apple, walnuts, spring onions, parsley, mayonnaise and black pepper to taste in a bowl and mix to combine. Place a layer of spinach leaves in base of bread case, top with a layer of chicken, a layer of apple mixture and finally a layer of tomato slices. Repeat layers, ending with a layer of spinach, until all ingredients are used and loaf is filled. Replace top and wrap loaf in aluminium foil. Place a board on top of loaf, weight down and refrigerate overnight. Serve cut into wedges.

Serves 8

A perfect picnic dish – delicate chicken breasts are combined with Waldorf salad ingredients, placed in a bread case, wrapped in aluminium foil and refrigerated overnight. All you have to do in the morning is pack the picnic basket and you are ready to go.

CRUSTY PARMESAN DRUMSTICKS

3 tablespoons Dijon mustard
4 tablespoons vegetable oil
4 spring onions, finely chopped
30 g/1 oz grated fresh Parmesan cheese
freshly ground black pepper
8 chicken drumsticks
1/2 cup/30 g/1 oz bread crumbs, made
from stale bread
60 g/2 oz butter, melted

1   Place mustard, oil, spring onions, Parmesan cheese and black pepper to taste in a bowl and mix to combine.

2   Brush each drumstick with mustard mixture, then roll in bread crumbs and place in a lightly greased baking dish. Pour butter over drumsticks and bake for 30 minutes or until drumsticks are cooked.

Serves 4

Oven temperature
180°C, 350°F, Gas 4

Crispy on the outside and moist inside, these drumsticks are a popular family meal. Serve with mashed potatoes and a green salad for one of the easiest meals you will ever make.

TURKEY CROQUETTES

90 g/3 oz butter
1$\frac{1}{3}$ cups/170 g/5$\frac{1}{2}$ oz flour
1 cup/250 mL/8 fl oz hot milk
125 g/4 oz ricotta cheese
250 g/8 oz cooked turkey, chopped
$\frac{1}{2}$ cup/60 g/2 oz grated tasty cheese
(mature Cheddar)
2 tablespoons chopped fresh parsley
1 cup/125 g/4 oz dried bread crumbs
1 egg, lightly beaten
oil for deep frying

1 Melt butter in a saucepan, stir in $\frac{1}{3}$ cup/45 g/1$\frac{1}{2}$ oz flour and cook, stirring, for 30 seconds. Whisk in milk and cook, stirring, over a medium heat for 4-5 minutes or until mixture thickens. Remove pan from heat and stir in ricotta cheese, turkey, tasty cheese (mature Cheddar) and parsley. Mix well to combine and refrigerate until completely cold.

2 Place bread crumbs and remaining flour on separate plates and set aside. Shape turkey mixture into croquette shapes, roll each croquette in flour, then dip in egg and roll in bread crumbs. Place on a plate lined with plastic food wrap, cover and chill for 15 minutes.

3 Heat oil in a large saucepan until hot and cook croquettes for 3-4 minutes or until golden.

Croquettes are a great way to use any leftover poultry or meat. In this recipe turkey has been used, but you could use leftover chicken, lamb or beef. Canned tuna or salmon are delicious alternatives. If using canned food, drain off any liquid first.

Turkey Croquettes

Serves 4

48

SUMMER CHICKEN SAUTE

2 tablespoons vegetable oil
1 onion, sliced
1 green pepper, cut into strips
1 red pepper, cut into strips
1 zucchini (courgette), sliced
$1^1/_2$ cups/375 mL/12 fl oz tomato purée
1 tablespoon chopped fresh basil
1 tablespoon chopped fresh parsley
1 teaspoon chopped fresh thyme or
$^1/_2$ teaspoon dried thyme
500 g/1 lb boneless chicken breast
fillets, cut into strips
freshly ground black pepper

1   Heat oil in a large frying pan and cook onion over a medium heat for 5 minutes or until soft. Add green and red pepper, zucchini (courgette) and tomato purée and bring to the boil, then reduce heat and simmer for 10 minutes.

2   Stir in basil, parsley, thyme and chicken and cook for 10 minutes or until chicken is cooked. Season to taste with black pepper.

Serves 4

A medley of summer vegetables and chicken makes a quick and easy sauté that is delicious served with boiled noodles tossed in butter and finely chopped fresh parsley.

Chicken with Curry Sauce

CHICKEN WITH CURRY SAUCE

Spatchcocking a bird means to split and flatten it. The easiest way to cut the bird is to use a pair of poultry shears. First cut off the wing tips then cut the bird along each side of the backbone to remove it. Now place the bird breast side up and using the heel of your hand push down sharply to flatten the bird and break the breastbone. To ensure that the bird holds its shape during cooking, thread two skewers through it. One skewer is threaded through the legs, avoiding the bones, and the other through the wings and breast.

60 g/2 oz butter
4 boneless chicken breast fillets, skin removed
1 onion, chopped
1 clove garlic, crushed
1 tablespoon curry powder
$^1/_2$ teaspoon ground cumin
$^1/_2$ teaspoon ground coriander
1 tablespoon honey
1 tablespoon fresh lemon juice
$^1/_3$ cup/90 mL/3 fl oz red wine
$^3/_4$ cup/185 mL/6 fl oz cream (double)
2 tablespoons mayonnaise
2 tablespoons chopped fresh coriander

Serves 4

1   Melt butter in a large frying pan and cook chicken over a medium heat for 3-4 minutes each side or until cooked. Remove chicken from pan, set aside and keep warm.

2   Add onion and garlic to pan and cook for 3-4 minutes or until onion is soft. Stir in curry powder, cumin and coriander, and cook for 2 minutes longer.

3   Stir in honey, lemon juice and wine, and cook for 2 minutes, then stir in cream and mayonnaise, and simmer for 2 minutes longer. Spoon sauce over chicken, sprinkle with coriander and serve immediately.

GRILLED HONEY CHICKEN

1 x 1.5 kg/3 lb chicken

HONEY GLAZE
3 tablespoons honey
2 teaspoons ground ginger
3 tablespoons Worcestershire sauce
2 tablespoons soy sauce
2 cloves garlic, crushed

1   Preheat grill to medium. Spatchcock chicken (see hint opposite) and place on a baking tray.

2   To make glaze, place honey, ginger, Worcestershire sauce, soy sauce and garlic in a small saucepan and bring to the boil over a medium heat. Brush glaze over chicken and cook under grill for 10-15 minutes each side or until chicken is cooked.

Grilled Honey Chicken

Serves 4

REDCURRANT SPATCHCOCK

Oven temperature
180°C, 350°F, Gas 4

2 spatchcocks (poussins),
cut in half lengthwise

REDCURRANT GLAZE
15 g/1 oz butter
4 tablespoons redcurrant jelly
2 teaspoons honey
3 tablespoons fresh lemon juice

1   To make glaze, place butter, redcurrant jelly, honey and lemon juice in a small saucepan and cook, stirring, over a medium heat until all ingredients are melted and combined.

2   Place spatchcocks (poussins) in a baking dish, brush with glaze and bake, occasionally brushing with glaze, for 25 minutes or until birds are cooked.

Serves 4

CHINESE CHICKEN WINGS

You might like to make baby drumsticks from the chicken wings. This makes them very easy to eat – especially for children or if serving as finger food.
To make baby drumsticks, first cut off the wings tips, then, holding the small end of the bone and using a sharp knife, cut around the bone to free the meat. Next cut, scrape and push meat down to large end of bone. Using your fingers pull the skin and meat down over end of bone so that the wing resembles a little drumstick.

60 g/2 oz butter
1 clove garlic, crushed
1 tablespoon grated fresh ginger
16 chicken wings
3 tablespoons honey
3 tablespoons Worcestershire sauce
3 tablespoons soy sauce
3 tablespoons sesame seeds

1   Melt butter in a large frying pan and cook garlic and ginger over a medium heat for 1 minute.

2   Add chicken wings and cook, stirring, for 3 minutes. Stir in honey, Worcestershire sauce and soy sauce and cook for 5 minutes longer or until chicken wings are cooked. Stir in sesame seeds and serve immediately.

Serves 4

Chinese Chicken Wings,
Redcurrant Spatchcock

Chicken Stroganoff

CHICKEN STROGANOFF

90 g/2 oz butter
500 g/1 lb boneless chicken breast
fillets, cut into strips
155 g/5 oz button mushrooms, halved
$^1/_2$ cup/125 mL/4 fl oz dry white wine
1 cup/250 mL/8 fl oz cream (double)
2 tablespoons tomato paste (purée)
$^1/_2$ teaspoon ground nutmeg
1 spring onion, finely chopped

1   Melt 60 g/2 oz butter in a large frying pan and cook chicken, stirring, over a medium heat for 2-3 minutes or until chicken just changes colour. Remove chicken from pan and set aside.

2   Melt remaining butter in pan and cook mushrooms for 2-3 minutes, then stir in wine, cream, tomato paste (purée) and nutmeg. Cook, stirring, over a high heat for 5 minutes or until sauce reduces and thickens slightly.

3   Add chicken to mushroom mixture and cook, stirring, over a medium heat, for 3-4 minutes or until chicken is cooked. Stir in spring onion and serve immediately.

Serves 4

Serve Chicken Stroganoff on a bed of boiled white or brown rice accompanied by a seasonal green vegetable – asparagus or green beans are delicious.

CHICKEN AND PIMENTO CASSEROLE

2 tablespoons vegetable oil
4 boneless chicken breast fillets,
cut into strips
1 turnip, cut into strips
2 onions, chopped
440 g/14 oz canned pimentos, drained
and cut into strips
1 cup/250 mL/8 fl oz dry white wine
440 g/14 oz canned tomatoes,
undrained and mashed
3 tablespoons chopped fresh basil

1   Heat oil in a large frying pan and cook chicken, stirring, over a medium heat for 2-3 minutes or until chicken just changes colour. Remove chicken from pan and set aside.

2   Add turnip, onions and pimentos to frying pan and cook for 3-4 minutes. Stir in wine and tomatoes and bring to the boil, stirring, over a medium heat, then reduce heat and simmer, uncovered, for 10 minutes or until turnip is tender. Return chicken to pan and cook for 3-4 minutes longer or until chicken is cooked. Stir in basil and serve immediately.

All this easy chicken dish needs to make a complete meal is hot garlic bread or crusty bread rolls and a salad of mixed lettuce and herbs.

Chicken and Pimento Casserole   **Serves 4**

VEGETABLE PAN-FRY

2 tablespoons vegetable oil
1 onion, chopped
1 green pepper, chopped
125 g/4 oz mushrooms, sliced
250 g/8 oz chicken livers, chopped
2 large tomatoes, peeled and chopped
2 fresh sage leaves, chopped
freshly ground black pepper
250 g/8 oz bow pasta, cooked

1   Heat oil in a large frying pan and cook onion for 3-4 minutes or until soft. Add green pepper and cook, stirring, for 3-4 minutes, then add mushrooms and cook for 2 minutes longer.

2   Add chicken livers and cook, stirring, for 3-4 minutes or until livers change colour. Stir in tomatoes, sage and black pepper to taste and cook, stirring constantly, for 4-5 minutes or until juice starts to run from tomatoes.

3   Add pasta to pan and cook for 4-5 minutes longer or until pasta is heated. Serve immediately.

Serves 4

A great way to use leftover pasta, this dish could be made using any small pasta shapes.

Vegetable Pan-fry

56

CHICKEN AND VEGETABLE PANCAKES

1 cup/125 g/4 oz flour
1 egg
1¹/₂ cups/375 mL/12 fl oz milk
1 zucchini (courgette), grated
2 tablespoons chopped fresh parsley

CHICKEN TOPPING
1 cup/250 mL/8 fl oz cream (double)
¹/₄ teaspoon ground nutmeg
¹/₄ cup/60 mL/2 fl oz white wine
250 g/8 oz cooked chicken, cut into pieces
1 tablespoon snipped fresh chives

1   Place flour, egg and milk in a food processor or blender and process until smooth. Transfer mixture to a bowl and stir in zucchini and parsley. Cover and set aside to stand for 15 minutes.

2   Pour enough mixture into a heated, greased small frying pan to just cover the base and cook over a medium-high heat, until bubbles form on the surface. Turn pancake and cook until golden brown. Repeat with remaining mixture.

3   To make topping, place cream in a saucepan and cook over a medium heat for 4-5 minutes or until cream is hot. Stir in nutmeg and wine and bring to simmering, then simmer for 10 minutes or until mixture reduces and thickens slightly. Stir in chicken and chives and cook for 2-3 minutes longer. To serve, spoon topping over pancakes.

Chicken and Vegetable Pancakes   **Serves 4**

For brunch, lunch or supper, pancakes are a great light meal. Grated zucchini (courgette) and chopped parsley in the batter make these pancakes deliciously different.

LEFTOVERS

Turkey is a must for Christmas and Thanksgiving. But what do you do with the leftovers? This selection of easy ideas will have you cooking turkey often, just so you can use the leftovers.

Turkey Tetrazzini

Turkey Creole

Turkey Noodle Bake

Turkey Hash

Quick Turkey Divan

Turkey and Feta Salad

Turkey Tetrazzini

Turkey Tetrazzini

90 g/3 oz plain tagliatelle
90 g/3 oz tomato tagliatelle
90 g/3 oz spinach tagliatelle
60 g/2 oz butter
4 rashers bacon, chopped
1 onion, chopped
125 g/4 oz mushrooms, sliced
$^1/_3$ cup/45 g/1$^1/_2$ oz flour
1$^3/_4$ cups/440 mL/14 fl oz chicken stock
$^3/_4$ cup/185 mL/6 fl oz cream (double)
2 tablespoons dry sherry
375 g/12 oz cooked turkey, cubed
pinch ground nutmeg
freshly ground black pepper
30 g/1 oz grated Parmesan cheese

1   Cook plain, tomato and spinach tagliatelle together in a large saucepan of boiling water following packet instructions. Drain, set aside and keep warm.

2   Melt butter in a saucepan and cook bacon and onion, stirring, over a medium heat for 4-5 minutes or until onion is soft. Add mushrooms and cook, stirring, for 5 minutes longer or until mushrooms are soft.

3   Stir in flour, then gradually stir in stock and bring to the boil. Reduce heat and simmer, stirring, for 4-5 minutes or until sauce thickens. Remove pan from heat and stir in cream, sherry, turkey, nutmeg, black pepper to taste and tagliatelle.

4   Spoon mixture into an ovenproof dish, sprinkle with Parmesan cheese and bake for 30 minutes or until top is golden.

Serves 4

Oven temperature
180°C, 350°F, Gas 4

When storing leftover turkey, remove the stuffing from the carcass and place in a separate bowl. Cover and refrigerate turkey and stuffing separately.

Turkey Creole

15 g/$^1/_2$ oz butter
1 clove garlic, crushed
1 onion, chopped
1 tablespoon flour
1 teaspoon chilli powder
$^1/_2$ cup/125 mL/4 fl oz tomato juice
$^1/_2$ cup/125 mL/4 fl oz chicken stock
375 g/12 oz cooked turkey, chopped
125 g/4 oz button mushrooms, sliced
freshly ground black pepper

1   Heat butter in a saucepan and cook garlic and onion over a medium heat for 3-4 minutes or until onion is soft. Stir in flour and chilli powder and cook, stirring, for 1 minute.

2   Stir in tomato juice and stock. Bring to the boil, stirring, over a medium heat, then reduce heat and simmer, stirring, until sauce thickens. Add turkey and mushrooms, season to taste with black pepper, bring to the boil, then reduce heat and simmer for 5 minutes.

Serves 4

Served on a bed of boiled rice, this makes a complete meal that is just right for the day after a feast.

TURKEY NOODLE BAKE

Oven temperature
180°C, 350°F, Gas 4

Remember cooked poultry is best used the next day and should always be used within two days of cooking.

375 g/12 oz egg noodles, cooked
250 g/8 oz cooked turkey, chopped
60 g/2 oz grated tasty cheese
(mature Cheddar)
2 stalks celery, chopped
2 cups/500 mL/16 fl oz milk
2 eggs
1 teaspoon curry powder
freshly ground black pepper
$1/2$ cup/30 g/1 oz bread crumbs,
made from stale bread
15 g/1 oz butter

1 Place one-third of noodles in base of a lightly greased ovenproof dish. Top with one-third each of turkey, cheese and celery. Repeat layers until all ingredients are used.

2 Place milk, eggs, curry powder and black pepper to taste in a bowl and whisk to combine. Carefully pour milk mixture over ingredients in dish, sprinkle with bread crumbs and dot with butter. Bake for 40 minutes or until firm.

Serves 6

TURKEY HASH

This tasty dish uses those foods that are most often leftover and turns them into something special. If you do not have leftover gravy, use cream of mushroom soup instead.

375 g/12 oz cooked turkey, chopped
2 potatoes, cooked and diced
1 cup/250 mL/8 fl oz leftover
turkey gravy
2 spring onions, chopped
freshly ground black pepper
4 slices wholegrain bread, toasted
and lightly buttered
2 tablespoons chopped fresh parsley

1 Place turkey, potatoes, gravy, spring onions and black pepper to taste in a saucepan and bring to the boil, stirring, over a medium heat.

2 Spoon turkey mixture over hot toast, sprinkle with parsley and serve immediately.

Serves 4

QUICK TURKEY DIVAN

4 slices bread, toasted and
lightly buttered
8 slices cooked turkey
375 g/12 oz canned asparagus
spears, drained
1 cup/250 mL/8 fl oz cream of
asparagus soup
1 cup/250 mL/8 fl oz evaporated milk
freshly ground black pepper
3 tablespoons grated fresh Parmesan
cheese

1 Place toast in base of a lightly greased, shallow ovenproof dish. Top with turkey slices and asparagus spears.

2 Place soup, milk and black pepper to taste in a bowl and mix to combine. Carefully pour soup mixture over ingredients in dish, sprinkle with Parmesan cheese and bake for 20-25 minutes or until top is golden and mixture bubbling.

Serves 4

Oven temperature
200°C, 400°F, Gas 6

TURKEY AND FETA SALAD

500 g/1 lb cooked turkey, cut into
bite-sized pieces
2 stalks celery, chopped
1 cucumber, peeled, seeded and chopped
12 black olives, pitted
250 g/8 oz feta cheese
1 bunch curly endive
1 small bunch watercress

BASIL VINAIGRETTE

1 clove garlic, crushed
4 tablespoons chopped fresh basil
2 tablespoons grain mustard
freshly ground black pepper
^{1}/4 cup/60 mL/2 fl oz fresh lemon juice
^{1}/4 cup/60 mL/2 fl oz red wine vinegar
^{1}/4 cup/60 mL/2 fl oz vegetable oil
^{1}/4 cup/60 mL/2 fl oz olive oil

1 To make vinaigrette, place garlic, basil, mustard, black pepper to taste, lemon juice, vinegar and vegetable and olive oils in a screwtop jar and shake well to combine.

2 Place turkey, celery, cucumber, olives and feta cheese in a bowl. Pour over vinaigrette and toss to combine.

3 Arrange endive leaves on four individual plates, top with salad and garnish with watercress. Serve immediately.

Serves 6 as a light meal

Serve this delicious one-dish salad with crusty rolls or bread for a complete meal.

FRENCH ROAST CHICKEN

Oven temperature
180°C, 350°F, Gas 4

1 x 1.5 kg/3 lb chicken
1 cup/250 mL/8 fl oz dry white wine
1 cup/250 mL/8 fl oz chicken stock
30 g/1 oz butter

CHEESE STUFFING
90 g/3 oz ricotta cheese
2 tablespoons chopped fresh parsley
2 teaspoons chopped fresh tarragon or
$^1/_2$ teaspoon dried tarragon leaves
4 spring onions, finely chopped
30 g/1 oz butter, softened
freshly ground black pepper

HERB STUFFING
60 g/2 oz butter
1 small onion, finely chopped
2 stalks celery, finely chopped
2 teaspoons chopped fresh tarragon or
$^1/_2$ teaspoon dried tarragon
2 tablespoons chopped fresh parsley
1 teaspoon finely grated lemon rind
2 cups/125 g/4 oz bread crumbs, made
from stale bread
freshly ground black pepper

GRAVY
$1^1/_2$ cups/375 mL/12 fl oz cooking
liquid and chicken stock
1 tablespoon cornflour
$^1/_2$ cup/125 mL/4 fl oz cream (double)
freshly ground black pepper

French Roast Chicken

Anthony Johnson/IMAGE BANK

1   To make Cheese Stuffing, place ricotta cheese, parsley, tarragon, spring onions, butter and black pepper to taste in a bowl and mix to combine.

2   Using your fingers, loosen skin on breast of chicken. Push Cheese Stuffing gently under skin, smoothing out evenly.

3   To make Herb Stuffing, melt butter in a saucepan and cook onion for 4-5 minutes or until soft. Place celery, tarragon, parsley, lemon rind and bread crumbs in a bowl, add onion mixture and mix to combine. Season to taste with black pepper. Spoon stuffing into cavity of chicken and secure neck end with metal or bamboo skewers.

4   Truss chicken and place breast side up on a wire rack set in a baking dish. Place wine, stock and butter in dish and bake chicken, turning and basting several times, for 1 hour or until skin is crisp and golden, and chicken is cooked. For the last 15 minutes of cooking, turn the chicken breast side up – this ensures that skin on the breast is crisp. Place chicken on a serving platter and set aside to rest in a warm place for 10 minutes before carving.

5   To make gravy, measure liquid in baking dish and, if necessary, make up to 1^{1}/2 cups/375 mL/12 fl oz with chicken stock. Return liquid to baking dish. Place dish on stove (cooker) top and bring to the boil over a medium heat. Place cornflour in a small bowl and whisk in cream. Whisk a little hot liquid into the cream mixture, then stir into baking dish. Cook, stirring constantly, for 3-4 minutes or until gravy boils and thickens. Season with black pepper. Serve gravy with chicken.

Serves 4

Paul E. Elson/IMAGE BANK

There should always be liquid in the base of the baking dish when roasting the chicken. If the liquid evaporates during cooking, add a little more wine or stock.

Paul E. Elson/IMAGE BANK

You might like to use blue cheese, cream cheese or Camembert in place of the ricotta cheese. If using Camembert, remove rind first.

TRUSSING A CHICKEN

Trussing a chicken helps it maintain its shape during cooking. Insert a metal skewer widthwise, just below the thigh bone, right through the body of the chicken. The ends of the skewer should be exposed either side. Place the chicken breast side down on a work surface. Take a length of string and catch in wing tips, then pass string under ends of skewer and cross over the back. Turn the chicken breast side up and tie in legs and the parson's nose.

CHICKEN WITH SPINACH FILLING

Oven temperature
180°C, 350°F, Gas 4

4 chicken marylands (uncut leg and
thigh joints)
30 g/1 oz butter, melted

SPINACH FILLING
125 g/4 oz frozen spinach, thawed
1 clove garlic, crushed
125 g/4 oz ricotta or cottage cheese,
drained
2 teaspoons grated Parmesan cheese
1 teaspoon finely grated lemon rind
pinch ground nutmeg

TOMATO SAUCE
310 g/10 oz canned tomato purée
2 teaspoons Worcestershire sauce

Chicken with Spinach Filling

1 To make filling, squeeze spinach to remove excess liquid. Place spinach, garlic, ricotta or cottage cheese, Parmesan cheese, lemon rind and nutmeg in a bowl and mix to combine.

2 Using your fingers, loosen skin on chicken, starting at thigh end.

3 Push filling gently under skin down into the drumstick. Arrange chicken pieces in an ovenproof dish, brush with melted butter and bake for 35-40 minutes.

4 To make sauce, place tomato purée and Worcestershire sauce in a saucepan, bring to simmering and simmer for 3-4 minutes. Serve sauce with chicken.

Serves 4

Drumsticks can be used in place of the chicken marylands if you wish.

Frozen chicken should be completely thawed before cooking. Thaw birds in refrigerator for 24-36 hours or in microwave on DEFROST (30%) for 10-15 minutes per 500 g/1 lb of chicken. Rinse cavity of chicken under cold running water to ensure that there are no remaining ice crystals.

SPICY CHICKEN PIES

Oven temperature
190°C, 375°F, Gas 5

PASTRY
3 cups/375 g/12 oz flour
90 g/3 oz butter, cut into pieces
90 g/3 oz lard, cut into pieces
$^1/_3$ cup/90 mL/3 fl oz cold water
1 egg, beaten

SPICY CHICKEN FILLING
30 g/1 oz butter
60 g/2 oz button mushrooms, chopped
1 onion, chopped
2 teaspoons garam masala
$^1/_4$ cup/30 g/1 oz flour
$^3/_4$ cup/185 mL/6 fl oz chicken stock
315 g/10 oz cooked chicken, diced
60 g/2 oz sweet corn kernels
freshly ground black pepper

1 To make filling, melt butter in a saucepan and cook mushrooms, onion and garam masala over a medium heat for 3-4 minutes or until onion is soft. Stir in flour and cook for 1 minute longer. Add stock and bring to the boil, stirring constantly. Reduce heat and simmer, stirring, for 2 minutes. Remove pan from heat, stir in chicken and sweet corn, season to taste with black pepper and set aside to cool completely.

Spicy Chicken Pies

2   To make pastry, place flour, butter and lard in a food processor and process until mixture resembles fine bread crumbs. With machine running, add water and process to form a firm dough. Turn dough onto a lightly floured surface and knead until smooth.

3   Take two-thirds of the dough and cut into four portions. Roll out each portion to fit a 12.5 cm/5 in loose-based, fluted flan tin. Line flan tins with pastry, press pastry into flutes, but do not trim top edge. Cut remaining pastry into four portions and roll out each portion to make a lid for each pie.

4   Spoon cold filling into flan tins. Dampen edges of pastry in tins and cover with pastry lids. Using a flat-bladed knife, press edges together to seal and cut off excess pastry. Gather together pastry trimmings, re-roll, then cut out pastry leaves and use to decorate tops of pies. Brush tops with beaten egg.

5   Place pies on a baking tray and bake for 40-45 minutes or until pastry is golden. Remove pies from oven and set aside to cool. When cool, remove from flan tins.

Serves 4

These pies are a delicious picnic food served with a fruit chutney and a crisp salad.

'Delicious as picnic fare or in a packed lunch, you will want to keep a supply of these pies in your freezer'

PERFECT ROAST TURKEY

Oven temperature
180°C, 350°F, Gas 4

4 kg/8 lb turkey
60 g/2 oz butter, melted
1 cup/250 mL/8 fl oz chicken stock

VEAL FORCEMEAT
30 g/1 oz butter
1 onion, finely chopped
1 rasher bacon, finely chopped
250 g/8 oz lean veal mince
3 cups/185 g/6 oz bread crumbs, made
from stale bread
$^1/_2$ teaspoon finely grated lemon rind
$^1/_2$ teaspoon finely chopped fresh parsley
$^1/_2$ teaspoon dried sage
pinch ground nutmeg
1 egg, lightly beaten
freshly ground black pepper

CHESTNUT STUFFING
440 g/14 oz canned chestnut purée,
sieved
2 cooking apples, cored, peeled
and grated
3 cups/185 g/6 oz bread crumbs,
made from stale bread
1 onion, finely chopped
1 stalk celery, finely chopped
4 tablespoons finely chopped walnuts
1 tablespoon finely chopped
fresh parsley
45 g/1$^1/_2$ oz butter, melted
1 egg, lightly beaten
pinch ground nutmeg
freshly ground black pepper

Perfect Roast Turkey

1   To make forcemeat, melt butter in a frying pan and cook onion and bacon for 4-5 minutes or until bacon is crisp. Add veal mince, bread crumbs, lemon rind, parsley, sage, nutmeg, egg and black pepper to taste. Mix well to combine.

2   To make stuffing, place chestnut purée, apples, bread crumbs, onion, celery, walnuts, parsley, butter, egg, nutmeg and black pepper to taste in a bowl and mix to combine.

3   Remove giblets and neck from turkey. Wipe turkey inside and out and dry well. Place stuffing in body cavity and lightly fill neck end of turkey with forcemeat. Secure openings with metal or bamboo skewers. Tuck wings under body of turkey and tie legs together.

4   Place turkey on a roasting rack in a baking dish. Brush with butter, then pour chicken stock into baking dish. Bake for 3-3$\frac{1}{2}$ hours or until tender. Baste frequently with pan juices during cooking. Set aside in a warm place to stand for 20 minutes before carving.

Serves 10

It is safest to defrost a frozen turkey in the refrigerator for 36-48 hours. Actual defrosting time will of course depend on the size of the bird. Once defrosted, wash bird and rinse out cavity, then pat dry using absorbent kitchen paper. Make sure that there are no ice crystals left in the cavity.

'Cooks have developed many wonderful turkey dishes for special occasions with delicious stuffings and accompaniments. Try this Roast Turkey for a Christmas or Thanksgiving dinner.'

CARVING THE TURKEY

A very sharp, pointed knife with a long flexible blade is best for carving turkey.
Before you start carving, remove string and skewers from bird and place breast
side up on a board or platter. Use a large carving fork to hold bird steady.

1 Removing first leg: Cut skin between thigh and breast of bird. Separate leg from body by bending thigh outwards to locate hip joint. Slice down through joint to remove the leg.

2 Separating thigh from drumstick: Hold knife at an angle between thigh and drumstick bones and cut firmly through joint to separate leg.

3 Slicing drumstick: Cut a thick slice of meat and skin from each side of drumstick, keeping knife close to the bone, then cut these into smaller slices.

4 Slicing thigh: Holding thigh steady, cut into four or more pieces, depending on the size of thigh. Repeat steps 1-4 for other leg of turkey.

5 Removing wing: Slice down through corner of breast towards wing. Push wing out to show joint and cut through joint. Remove wing with piece of breast attached.

6 Carving breast: Holding breast steady, slice down through meat. When you reach incision above the wing joint, the slice will fall free.

COOKING TIMES FOR A STUFFED TURKEY

Cook turkeys at 180°C/350°F/Gas 4. If cooked in a hotter oven the outside of the bird browns and cooks before the centre.

Weight	Time
2.5-3 kg/5-6 lb	2$\frac{1}{2}$-3 hours
3-4 kg/6-8 lb	3-3$\frac{1}{2}$ hours
4-6 kg/8-12 lb	3$\frac{1}{2}$-4 hours

CHICKEN STOCK

4 whole cloves
2 onions, halved crossways
1 chicken carcass, skin removed and
trimmed of
all visible fat
12 cups/3 litres/5 pt cold water
2 carrots, roughly chopped
4 stalks celery, roughly chopped
fresh herbs of your choice
$^1/_2$ teaspoon black peppercorns

1 Stick cloves into onion halves.

2 Place chicken carcass, water, carrots, celery, herbs, peppercorns and clove-studded onions in a large saucepan. Bring to the boil, reduce heat and simmer, stirring occasionally, for 2 hours.

3 Strain stock and refrigerate overnight. Skim fat from surface of stock and use as required.

Makes 8 cups/2 litres/3$^1/_2$ pt

The microwave is particularly good for making small quantities of stock. To make stock in the microwave, place chicken carcass remaining after a roast or raw carcass, 1 chopped onion, 1 chopped carrot, 2 stalks chopped celery, parsley and thyme in a large microwave-safe container. Add water to cover ingredients. Cook, uncovered, on HIGH (100%) for 45 minutes. Strain stock and refrigerate overnight. Skim fat from the surface and use as required.

Chicken stock is the basis of many classic dishes.
Stock will keep in the refrigerator for 3-4 days, or in the freezer
for 12 months. Freeze stock in $^1/_2$ cup/125 mL/4 fl oz or
1 cup/250 mL/8 fl oz portions for easy use at a later date.

CRUSTY CHICKEN GOULASH

Oven temperature
180°C, 350°F, Gas 4

2 tablespoons vegetable oil
2 large onions, chopped
1¹/₂ tablespoons paprika
2 tablespoons seasoned flour
500 g/1 lb boneless chicken breast
fillets, cut into strips
1 tablespoon tomato paste (purée)
¹/₂ cup/125 mL/4 fl oz red wine
¹/₂ cup/125 mL/4 fl oz chicken stock
3 tablespoons natural yogurt

SOUR CREAM CRUST
125 g/4 oz butter, softened
300 g/9¹/₂ oz sour cream
1 egg
1 cup/125 g/4 oz self-raising flour, sifted
1 tablespoon chopped fresh parsley

Crusty Chicken Goulash

1   Heat 1 tablespoon oil in a large frying pan and cook onions, stirring, over a medium heat for 5-6 minutes or until golden. Remove onions from pan and set aside. Combine paprika and flour in a plastic food bag, add chicken, shake to coat with flour mixture, then shake off excess flour mixture.

2   Heat remaining oil in frying pan and cook chicken, stirring, over a medium heat for 2-3 minutes. Return onions to pan, stir in tomato paste (purée), wine and stock. Bring to the boil, stirring constantly, then reduce heat, cover and simmer for 6-7 minutes. Remove pan from heat, stir in yogurt and set aside to cool.

3   To make crust, place butter, sour cream and egg in a bowl. Stir in flour and parsley and mix well to combine.

4   To assemble, place crust mixture in an 8 cup/2 litre/3^1/$_2$ pt lightly greased casserole dish and work mixture to cover sides and base of dish.

5   Spoon filling into crust, cover with lid of dish and bake for 35 minutes. Remove lid and bake for 10 minutes longer.

Serve this delicious chicken with a tossed green salad or a boiled, steamed or microwaved green vegetable such as green beans, zucchini (courgettes), snow peas (mangetout) or asparagus.

Serves 4

'*A chicken goulash surrounded by a rich sour cream crust is just the thing for that special occasion.*'

CHICKEN LIVER PATE

60 g/2 oz butter
1 onion, finely chopped
1 clove garlic, crushed
250 g/8 oz chicken livers, chopped
1-2 teaspoons curry powder
$^{1}/_{2}$ cup/125 mL/4 fl oz chicken stock
2 hard-boiled eggs, cut
into wedges
freshly ground black pepper
cayenne pepper
fresh bay leaves
lemon slices

1   Melt 30 g/1 oz butter in a frying pan and cook onion, garlic and chicken livers, stirring, over a medium heat for 5 minutes. Add curry powder and cook for 1 minute longer. Add stock and cook, stirring, for 5 minutes. Remove pan from heat and set aside to cool for 10 minutes.

2   Place chicken liver mixture and eggs in a food processor or blender and blend to form a smooth purée.

3   Season to taste with black and cayenne pepper. Spoon pâté into a terrine and smooth surface. Melt remaining butter and pour over pâté. Decorate with bay leaves and lemon slices. Refrigerate for several hours. Serve with biscuits or crusty bread.

MICROWAVING POULTRY

As poultry has a low fat content it does not brown naturally when cooked in the microwave, so use a baste or browning agent to add colour and flavour.

The following hints will ensure your microwaved birds are perfect:

🍂 Before cooking, tuck wings under bird and tie legs together using a rubber band or string. (Rubber bands do not melt if you use them in the microwave.)

🍂 Start cooking bird, breast side down and turn over halfway through cooking.

🍂 If you wish your bird to have a roasted appearance and taste do not cover during cooking, as covering causes the bird to steam. Cooking a bird in a covered casserole is the ideal way to cook it if you wish to use the flesh in a soup or for chicken salad.

🍂 A stuffed bird will take a little longer to cook. Add 2 minutes to the total cooking time.

🍂 Cook birds elevated on a roasting rack.

🍂 For larger birds, such as turkeys, you may need to shield the wings and drumsticks with aluminium foil during cooking.

🍂 On completion of cooking, cover bird with aluminium foil and allow to stand for 10-15 minutes.

🍂 For those working in metric measures, an easy way to calculate the cooking time of a chicken is to take its weight, remove the decimal point and cook for that many minutes each side. For example, you would cook a 1.5 kg chicken for 15 minutes each side – a total cooking time of 30 minutes. You can use a similar formula for cooking other poultry, but remember to cook turkey for the first 10 minutes on HIGH (100%) then reduce the power setting to MEDIUM-HIGH (70%).

Chicken cooks quickly in the microwave and is moist and tender.

MICROWAVE COOKING CHART

FOOD	POWER LEVEL	COOKING TIMES per 500 g/1 lb
Whole chicken	HIGH (100%)	10 minutes
Chicken pieces	HIGH(100%)	10 minutes
Turkey	HIGH (100%)	10 minutes then
	MEDIUM-HIGH (70%)	10 minutes
Quail	HIGH (100%)	8 minutes
Duck	HIGH (100%)	10 minutes
Goose	MEDIUM-HIGH (70%)	12 minutes

CHICKEN

What distinguishes a spatchcock (poussin) from a chicken? Read on and find out the differences between the various types of birds and what to look for when buying. As part of an everyday diet, chicken is a delicious and healthy food. Most of its fat lies just under the skin, which is easily removed for low-fat cooking.

Whether it's a simple family meal or a formal dinner party, chicken has a place. In recent years its increased availability and moderate price has taken it from being a luxury food to one that can be included regularly as part of your diet.

BUYING: Whole chickens are available fresh or frozen, in a variety of sizes. When buying fresh chicken the bird should have a fresh smell; an unbroken skin with no dark patches; the breast should be plump; the tip of the breastbone soft and pliable; and there should be little moisture on the bird.

Chicken is also sold in pieces – the breast being the most tender and the leanest. Breast chicken is frequently sold as boneless breast fillets which are suitable for poaching, baking, grilling and pan cooking. The dark meat on the thighs and drumsticks is higher in fat. The uncut thigh and drumstick portion is called a chicken maryland and is popular crumbed and baked. The wings in small and average-sized birds have little meat but make great finger food when marinated and grilled, baked or barbecued. They are also often used in soups.

SPATCHCOCK (POUSSIN): A spatchcock, or poussin, is a very small chicken about 6 weeks old and weighing 500 g-1 kg/1-2 lb. Usually one bird per serving is allowed. It is very tender with a delicate flavour that makes it particularly suited to roasting, pot roasting, casseroling, grilling and barbecuing.

SPRING CHICKEN: Slightly larger and a little older than a spatchcock (poussin), a spring chicken is about 8 weeks old and weighs about 1 kg/2 lb. One bird serves two people.

BOILING FOWLS: This is an older hen (often 18 months or older) that has stopped laying. It is tough and needs a moist method of cooking. The best way to cook a boiling fowl is to boil or stew it. The cooking time will be about 3 hours, and vegetables are added towards the end of the cooking.

TURKEY: Turkey is available in many guises. Whole birds vary greatly in size from around 2.5 kg/5 lb to as large as 13.5 kg/30 lb. Other cuts, such as turkey buffe – which is the breast with the bone in – rolled breast and fillets are also available and have the advantage of being easier to carve. Turkey hindquarters are also an economic and tasty alternative. Turkey is a nutritious low-fat food; in fact it has half the fat and a third of the cholesterol of domestic chicken.

DUCK: Duck has a similar nutrient content to chicken but has twice as much fat. To remove some of the fat during cooking, duck is often cooked on a rack set in a baking dish.

Farmed duck is available both fresh and frozen and should have creamy-white skin with a plump breast. A duck is a bird that is 2-3 months old, weighing 2-3 kg/4-6 lb, while a duckling is a smaller, younger duck of 6-8 weeks, weighing 1.5-2 kg/3-4 lb. Wild duck varies greatly in size, age and taste, and requires a moist method of cooking for best results.

QUAIL: Quail is now widely available and is a popular gourmet food. It has a delicate flesh and care should be taken during cooking to prevent it drying out. The average bird weighs 155 g/5 oz and is delicious roasted, braised, pan-cooked or made into pies and pâtés.

STORAGE: The same basic rules apply to all poultry and game birds.

A fresh bird should be removed from its wrapping and placed on a plate then covered lightly so that air can circulate around it.

If preparing the bird in advance, do not stuff it until just prior to cooking. However, the stuffing and the bird can be prepared in advance and stored separately.

To avoid the possibility of salmonella food poisoning, it is important to completely defrost a frozen bird before cooking. To defrost, leave the frozen bird in its original wrapping and place in the refrigerator for 24 hours or longer, depending on its size. Defrosting can also be done in the microwave using DEFROST (30%) and allowing 10 minutes per 500 g/1 lb.

USEFUL INFORMATION

QUICK CONVERTER

Metric	Imperial
5 mm	$^1/_4$ in
1 cm	$^1/_2$ in
2 cm	$^3/_4$ in
2.5 cm	1 in
5 cm	2 in
10 cm	4 in
15 cm	6 in
20 cm	8 in
23 cm	9 in
25 cm	10 in
30 cm	12 in

MEASURING LIQUIDS

Metric	Imperial	Cup
30 mL	1 fl oz	
60 mL	2 fl oz	$^1/_4$ cup
90 mL	3 fl oz	
125 mL	4 fl oz	$^1/_2$ cup
155 mL	5 fl oz	
170 mL	$5^1/_2$ fl oz	$^2/_3$ cup
185 mL	6 fl oz	
220 mL	7 fl oz	
250 mL	8 fl oz	1 cup
500 mL	16 fl oz	2 cups
600 mL	20 fl oz (1 pt)	
750 mL	$1^1/_4$ pt	
1 litre	$1^3/_4$ pt	4 cups
1.2 litres	2 pt	

METRIC CUPS & SPOONS

Metric	Cups	Imperial
60 mL	$^1/_4$ cup	2 fl oz
80 mL	$^1/_3$ cup	$2^1/_2$ fl oz
125 mL	$^1/_2$ cup	4 fl oz
250 mL	1 cup	8 fl oz
Spoons		
1.25 mL	$^1/_4$ teaspoon	
2.5 mL	$^1/_2$ teaspoon	
5 mL	1 teaspoon	
20 mL	1 tablespoon	

MEASURING DRY INGREDIENTS

Metric	Imperial
15 g	$^1/_2$ oz
30 g	1 oz
60 g	2 oz
90 g	3 oz
125 g	4 oz
155 g	5 oz
185 g	6 oz
220 g	7 oz
250 g	8 oz
280 g	9 oz
315 g	10 oz
375 g	12 oz
410 g	13 oz
440 g	14 oz
470 g	15 oz
500 g	16 oz (1 lb)
750 g	1 lb 8 oz
1 kg	2 lb
1.5 kg	3 lb

OVEN TEMPERATURES

°C	°F	Gas Mark
120	250	$^1/_2$
140	275	1
150	300	2
160	325	3
180	350	4
190	375	5
200	400	6
220	425	7
240	475	8
250	500	9

In this book, ingredients such as fish and meat are given in grams so you know how much to buy. It is handy to have:

❧ A small inexpensive set of kitchen scales.

Other ingredients in our recipes are given in tablespoons and cups, so you will need:

❧ A nest of measuring cups (1 cup, $^1/_2$ cup, $^1/_3$ cup and $^1/_4$ cup).

❧ A set of measuring spoons (1 tablespoon, 1 teaspoon, $^1/_2$ teaspoon and $^1/_4$ teaspoon).

❧ A transparent graduated measuring jug (1 litre or 250 mL) for measuring liquids.

❧ Cup and spoon measures are level.

INDEX

Almond Chicken Rolls 16
Avocado
   and Chicken Soup 5
   Sandwiches, Grilled 45
   Strudel 28
Bacon
   and Chicken Liver Kebabs 41
   and Mushroom Rolls 9
Basil
   Mayonnaise 35
   Vinaigrette 61
Bean and Chicken Bake 17
Black Olive Stuffing 19
Blueberry Duck 20
Burgers, Healthy Chicken 42
Buttermilk Muffins with Turkey 44
Cheese Stuffing 62
Cherry Sauce 8
Chestnut Stuffing 68
Chicken
   see also Spatchcock
   Breast
      Almond Rolls 16
      Avocado Strudel 28
      Chilli, with Curry Sauce 8
      Coconut Curry 13
      Crusty Goulash 72
      with Curry Sauce 50
      Mango Bites 7
      Marsala 20
      Oriental Stir-fry 22
      and Pimento Casserole 55
      Pimento Pie 24
      Pot Pie 30
      Roll Casserole 25
      Rolls, Oriental 7
      Satay 10
      Spicy Indian 11
      Stroganoff 54
      Summer Sauté 49
      Waldorf Loaf 47
   Cooked
      and Avocado Soup 5
      Curry Soup 3
      Grilled Avocado Sandwiches 44

Noodle Soup 4
   and Orange Salad 37
   and Pepper Tortillas 43
   Soup, Creamy 3
   Spicy Pies 66
   and Tomato Salad 35
   and Vegetable Pancakes 57
   Warm Oriental Salad 36
Drumsticks
   with Corn 14
   Crusty Parmesan 47
   Feta 13
Marylands with Spinach
   Filling 64
Mince
   Burgers 42
   Tacos 41
Pieces
   Bean Bake 17
   Biryani 29
Smoked, Salad 35
Stock 71
Whole
   Chickpea Ragout 32
   French Roast 62
   Grilled Honey 51
   Herb Chutney 23
   Rice-filled 14
   Terrine 27
Wings, Chinese 52
Chicken Liver
   Bacon and Mushroom Rolls 9
   and Bacon Kebabs 41
   Pâté 74
   and Spinach Salad 38
   Vegetable Pan-fry 56
Chickpea Ragout 32
Chilli Chicken with Curry Sauce 8
Chinese Chicken Wings 52
Chutney Stuffing 23
Coconut Curry 13
Courgette Flowers 20
Croquettes, Turkey 48
Cucumber Coriander Dip 11
Curry
   Chicken Soup 3
   Coconut 13
   Sauce 8
   Sauce with Chicken 50
   Spicy Indian Chicken 11
Dressing
   Basil Mayonnaise 35

Basil Vinaigrette 61
Creamy Onion 39
Peanut 36
Tarragon 37
Watercress 35
Duck
   Blueberry 20
   with Cherry Sauce 8
   Honey-glazed 18
   Redcurrant 32
   Roast, Salad 39
Feta
   Drumsticks 13
   and Turkey Salad 61
French Roast Chicken 62
Fruity Smoked Chicken Salad 35
Herb
   Butter 16
   Chutney Chicken 23
   Spatchcock 31
   Stuffing 62
Honey
   Chicken 51
   Glazed Duck 18
   Roast Quail 26
Indian Chicken 11
Kebabs, Bacon and Chicken
   Liver 41
Loaf, Chicken Waldorf 47
Mango Chicken Bites 7
Marinade, Herb Butter 31
Mayonnaise, Basil 35
Muffins, Buttermilk, with
   Turkey 44
Mushroom Sauce 14
Noodle
   and Chicken Soup 4
   Turkey Bake 60
Olive
   Rice 22
   Stuffing 19
Onion Dressing 39
Oriental Chicken Rolls 7
Oriental Stir-fry 22
Pancakes, Chicken and
   Vegetable 57
Parmesan Drumsticks 47
Pâté
   Chicken Liver 74
   Chicken Terrine 27
Peanut Dressing 36
Pie

Chicken Pot 30
Pimento Chicken 24
Spicy Chicken 66
Pimento Chicken Pie 24
Plum Sauce 7
Polenta Pastry 24
Poussin *see* Spatchcock
Quail
    Honeyed Roast 26
    with Olive Rice 22
Redcurrant
    Duck 32
    Spatchcock 52
Rice
    Filled Chicken 14
    Olive 22
    Pilau 29
Salad
    Chicken and Orange 37
    Chicken Waldorf Loaf 47
    Creamy Roast Duck 39
    Fruity Smoked Chicken 35
    Spinach and Chicken Liver 38
    Tomato and Chicken 35
    Turkey and Feta 61
    Warm Oriental Chicken 36
Sandwiches, Grilled Avocado 45
Satay Chicken 10

Smoked Chicken Salad 35
Soup
    Chicken and Avocado 5
    Chicken Noodle 4
    Creamy Chicken 3
    Curried Chicken 3
Soy Honey Glaze 26
Spatchcock
    Herbed 31
    with Olives 19
    Redcurrant 52
Spicy Indian Chicken 11
Spinach and Chicken Liver
    Salad 38
Stir-fry, Oriental 22
Stock, Chicken 71
Strudel, Avocado 28
Stuffing
    Black Olive 19
    Cheese 62
    Chestnut 68
    Chutney 23
    Herb 62
    Veal Forcemeat 68
Tacos, Chicken 41
Tarragon Dressing 37
Terrine, Chicken 27
Tomato

and Chicken Salad 35
    Sauce 64
Tortillas, Chicken and Pepper 43
Turkey
    and Buttermilk Muffins 44
    Creole 59
    Croquettes 48
    Divan 61
    and Feta Salad 61
    Hash 60
    Noodle Bake 60
    Perfect Roast 68
    Tetrazzini 59
Veal Forcemeat 68
Vegetable Pan-fry 56
Warm Oriental Chicken Salad 36
Watercress Dressing 35
Zucchini Flowers 20

UK COOKERY EDITOR
Katie Swallow

EDITORIAL
Food Editor: Rachel Blackmore
Editorial Assistant: Ella Martin
Editorial Co-ordinator: Margaret Kelly
Recipe Development: Sheryle Eastwood, Carolyn Fienberg, Joanne
Glynn, Lucy Kelly, Anneka Mitchell, Penelope Peel, Belinda Warn,
Loukie Werle
Credits: Recipes pages 66, 74 by Louise Steel; pages 4, 56, 59 by
Lesley Mackley; pages 8, 9 by Lorna Rhodes © Merehurst Limited

PHOTOGRAPHY
Simon Butcher, Per Ericson, Paul Grater, Ashley Mackevicius,
Harm Mol, Yanto Noerianto, Andrew Payne, Jon Stewart,
Warren Webb

STYLING
Wendy Berecry, Belinda Clayton, Carolyn Fienberg, Anna Philips,
Jacqui Hing, Michelle Gorry

DESIGN AND PRODUCTION
Manager: Sheridan Carter
Layout: Lulu Dougherty
Design: Frank Pithers
Finished Art: Stephen Joseph

Published by J.B. Fairfax Press Pty Limited
Formatted by J.B. Fairfax Press Pty Limited
Output by Adtype, Sydney
Printed by Toppan Printing Co, Singapore

© J.B. Fairfax Press Pty Limited, 1993
This book is copyright. No part may be reproduced or transmitted
without the written permission of the publisher. Enquiries should be
made in writing to the publisher.

170 UK
Includes Index
ISBN 1 86343 045 8 (pbk)
ISBN 1 85391 283 2

Distributed by J.B. Fairfax Press Ltd
9 Trinity Centre, Park Farm Estate
Wellingborough, Northants, UK
Ph: (0933) 402330 Fax: (0933) 402234